Published by Lulu Books.

Lulu Books, Raleigh, N.C. USA.

www.lulu.com

First published by Brian Stretton in 2014.

Copyright © Brian. W. Stretton, 2014. All rights reserved.

The moral right of the author has been asserted.

Except in the United States, this book is sold subject to the condition that it shall not, by way of trade or otherwise, be lent, re-sold, hired out, or otherwise circulated without the publisher's prior consent in any binding form of binding cover other than that in which it is published and without a similar condition including this condition being imposed on the subsequent purchaser.

978-1-326-10481-8

During his acceptance speech for the Nobel Prize for economics in 2002, Vernon Smith said

"I urge students to read narrowly within economics, but widely in science. Within economics there is essentially only one model.... the economic literature is not the best place to find new inspiration beyond these traditional technical models of modelling."

I find the same limitation within Health and Safety literature and urge those interested in how to improve Safety management and performance to be as open minded and progressive in their endeavour.

Contents

Introduction — Page 11

Section One: Behavioural Safety and the theory that all accidents are preventable

    The model of the year — Page 19
    Safety people — Page 30
    Behavioural Safety — Page 45
    How behaviour affects Safety — Page 50
    The importance of a belief — Page 58
    Conscious and unconscious actions — Page 62

Section Two: The flaw in the theory and what we can do about it

    The elephant in the corner — Page 69
    What do you mean 'rational'? — Page 73
    How much of an island are we on? — Page 79
    Noel, Isaac, John and Herb — Page 83
    Achieving cultural change — Page 89
    Bill Bratten: Super-cop — Page 94
    The tragic case of Elaine Bromiley — Page 106
    The story of Sir Chris Hoy and a frog — Page 116

Section Three: Soft power; Safety nudges

    What is 'nudge'? — Page 125
    What makes humans likely to take risks? — Page 130
    The importance of a belief — Page 136
    Ones and zeros baby — Page 141
    The man with two brains — Page 145
    Sheep, smiles and frowns — Page 151
    Exercising Homer — Page 157
    What time is it? — Page 163

Final thoughts — Page 167

Things to see or read — Page 175

About the Author

Brian Stretton

Ma HSEL CMIOSH MIIRSM RMaPs MinstLM

On leaving school I worked as a as a trainee supervisor with my employing sponsor Tarmac Construction Ltd (Carillion as it is now in 2014).

I attended the National Construction College at CITB (Construction Industry Trade Board) Bircham Newton, Norfolk on their residential 12 month civil engineering course. The CITB, for the non-initiated, is the organising authority for the construction sector. They have centres across the country with their headquarters being Bircham Newton.

From that point I worked on various major civil engineering projects around the UK gaining experience in a tough, but enjoyable career. As the travelling and living associated with this type of work can be excessive, I decided to move into the material supply industry which enabled me to be based from home. An opportunity arrived in 1989 for me to join the CITB, this time as their civil engineering trainer instead of a trainee. I stayed with CITB for 13 years and during this tenancy of employ I progressed to becoming Safety training advisor for the west region of England and Wales. This is where I became involved in the world of Health and Safety. Aware of the risk of becoming completely institutionalised, I left the Safety of 'The Board' and re-joined the world of contracting with Birse as their Safety Training Manager, which later became part of the Balfour Beatty Group. Here I created and developed their Health and Safety training provision and completed my journey from boots to boardroom as Director of Safety Training. The final chapter of my career has seen me leave the corridors of power that a major contractor such as Balfour Beatty create to work independently as a consultant and proprietor of my own limited company, delivering services to industry in all matters of Health and Safety as well as advice in legal matters.

At the time of writing I have been in the construction industry for 40 years. I have been married for 36 years to my wife Pam and we have two children, Shelley and Paul who also work in our Health and Safety Company.

When not practising Health and Safety I can be found playing enjoyable, but low standard golf, appreciating the hospitality that the local pub can offer or watching any sport that happens to be on TV at the time.

Enjoy the book.

Introduction

It seems a little unusual these days to start an introduction to a Safety based event and not open with the usual domestics. I shall have to presume that you are aware of the procedures in place in the event a fire alarm is raised whilst you are reading this book and that you know where the facilities are for you to have a drink and make yourself comfortable. It is even stranger for me not to have to ask you politely to turn your phone to silent whilst reading. Having said that, before proceeding any further I would advise you to ensure that all this information is familiar to you.

I am not a book-read Safety professional. I have experienced Health and Safety as an operative, supervisor, manager and director. I know the issues and the problems within it. This shall not be a Safety book written by a brilliant academic, but by someone with experience of how Health and Safety exists across the industry on a day to day basis. You will find models and theories at some points with reference to academic works, but I shall try not to dazzle with overly scientific or academic language. I want this to be real. This is not a 'Safety chat' from an old boy, but aims to bridge the divide between theoretical academic approaches to Health and Safety and the challenges that people face regarding implementation and management of Health and Safety on the shop floor. In short, this shall be an honest account of the Safety profession based on years of experience in various guises and hopes to give you something that can be taken away and used within your organisations.

Over my many years I have been attributed many adjectives. Most of them pleasant, but some are less so, for which I predominantly have my two children to thank. However, one aspect of my personality that does crop up is my ambition. Not the naked, overt ambition that would gain me a place on The Apprentice, but a quiet drive to succeed and improve.

This book shares my ambitious outlook and approach to things. The first section shall offer a short over view of behavioural Safety concepts and an introduction to human factors. I am aware that people reading this may well already have an exposure to this subject and so do not wish to simply revisit familiar material, but want to ensure that the key messages within this book are just as accessible to the non-initiated.

The second section will delve more deeply into Safety at the macro level. Primarily how can we change an organisations Safety culture. This is a more strategic, abstract level for an organisation or group wishing to explore ways in which to enable change and progress. It shall also offer some observations, based on the latest academic research, to the established rationale as it stands regarding behavioural approaches to Safety.

The final section works at the micro level; the individual. In particular how can we gain greater understanding of decision making and how we can try to use this understanding to more effectively shape Safety performance? Ultimately; how can we make a difference?

And so with no further ado I would like to start on our first area of discussion: Behavioural Safety and the theory that all accidents are preventable.

Section One:

Behavioural Safety and the theory that all accidents are preventable

The Model of the Year

Welcome to my first paradox. How can a man that believes that good Health and Safety doesn't require the use of a quantity of paper sufficient to publish a daily newspaper commit to writing a book, in the knowledge that the process will fell a couple of Giant Redwoods? During my last years of working within Health and Safety I have spent most of my time talking. To find myself writing instead feels a little peculiar. I do hope that through this book I shall take you on a journey. A slightly convoluted journey at times with detours that you may not expect, but with the firm hope that both the destination as well as the journey itself will reveal themselves to be worthwhile.

To enable us to begin our journey it is therefore necessary to look at where we are currently with Health and Safety and where we want to head to. In order to consider these questions as well as identify some of the challenges that we may face along the way, I shall introduce the Model of the Year.

At this point, I must apologise to people that saw the heading of this section and thought that this truly was a different type of Health and Safety book. The model of the year I refer to in this section is not one similar to the models that used to adorn the many site offices that I used to work out of. Whilst that was considered, I didn't want it to distract from the key messages of the section or encourage any readers to lose focus.

The model of the year does not claim to be revolutionary. Indeed it exists in various guises in management text books. The first version that I came across was by Baddeley and James. Over the years I have redesigned this model using a variety of metaphors and characters, right through from a water-well to Darth Vader. Whatever form it takes though, I find it resonates with the audience and is able to be applied at different perspectives. And that is precisely what I intent to do now as we begin to build up our understanding of the Health and Safety as a whole, where we are, and to consider where we want to go.

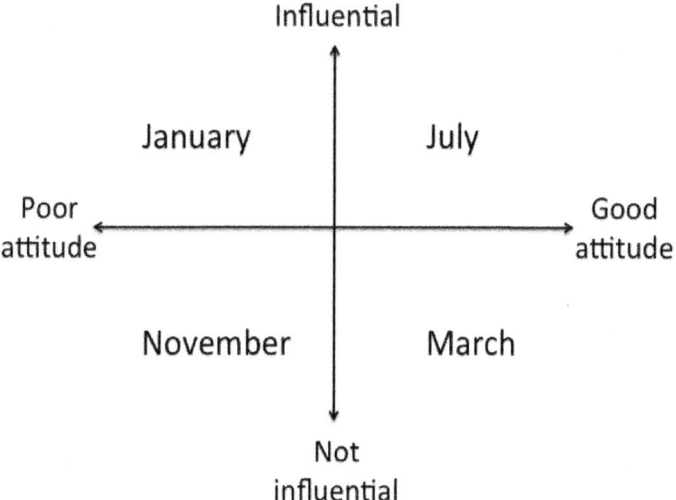

The model has two axes. The horizontal axis is used to determine an individual's attitude towards Health and Safety. So somebody that has a very positive attitude towards Safety would be towards the right hand side of the model and would progressively move leftwards as their attitude towards Safety becomes more negative.

The vertical axis considers a person's level influence within a given group or dynamic. This does not simply refer to status within a company or job title, but also their personal skills. If a person was considered to be very influential they would be positioned near to the top of the model and move progressively down the axis as they become progressively less influential.

Once those two factors are considered, a cross can be placed on the model which best describes their levels of both attitude and influence regarding Health and Safety within the workplace, much in the same manner one would select the place of the football in the "Spot the Ball" competitions I used to do each Saturday morning. For example, a person that considered themselves to have a largely positive attitude towards Safety, but is not particularly influential would find themselves in the bottom right hand square of the model.

I have chosen this incarnation of the model as a calendar year as I find it is universally intuitive. I shall apportion each corner to a particular month and use this as a basis to depict the typical scene for that month and anticipate that certain feelings and perceptions will automatically be evoked within the reader. With the backdrop set, I will then develop each month into how it relates to people within the workplace as a whole as well as the Health and Safety profession.

It is July. It's a warm 24 degrees and has been for a week or so. It is bright first thing in the morning and remains so for many hours after work in which it is possible to spend some time doing some more enjoyable things; gardening, a game of golf or relax in a local beer garden. The summer holidays loom large andthe ice cream van passes routinely much to the excitement of the local children. There is no suggestion of a hosepipe ban, or of it being so uncomfortably warm people can't sleep well enough. There is even a decent possibility of a strong home nation showing in the football tournament and a British winner at Wimbledon. Much like the summer of 2012 really, apart from better weather and a more optimistic prognosis regarding the football.

Safety July is the pinnacle. The ideal. It is consistent and positive. The main challenge for Safety July is to make sure everything remains sunny in the garden. That the mornings are not clouded or foggy, and the weekends aren't spoilt by a bout of rain. To ensure complacency does not creep in quietly, else the wonderful summer shall quickly subside and it shall soon be the onset of autumn; in Safety speak; badness.

It is March. It arrives after months of scraping off the frost from the windscreen and the last time anyone saw daylight seems like an implausibly long time ago. The grass begins to grow and requires work and support, but the smell of it freshly cut is more of a positive externality. The sun has rolled out from under its large duvet and occasionally smiles down on you. The sense of optimism rises and a sense of summer looming replaces the hat and scarf which have now been put back in a cupboard somewhere. In nine months from now, when there are many drunken revellers singing Auld Lang Syne to the chimes of Big Ben, very few will look back fondly at March – especially given the glorious, perfect summer that was July, however, March had all the promise and potential.

As a Safety professional I like Safety March. It is positive and optimistic. It may require some support and guidance, but with the right help Safety March can usher in the golden summer of July. Like those buds shooting up out of the soil I am conscious of the surprise exposure to a ground frost, which can stump any growth or Safety culture potential.

Ideally I would like everyone to range between Safety March and Safety July, from the optimistic potential to the sunny icon to which we aspire. Whether they are able to offer the leadership and guidance or require it is a crucial and important management function, but if everyone occupies themselves in this area then I know my job, premises or site shall be highly productive, profitable, on time, and safe. Unfortunately in the real world not everyone fits within this 'goldilocks' zone.

It is November and it has started to get cold. Really, very cold. And your hat and scarf are definitely not in the same cupboard in which you left them earlier in the year. The mornings are dark. The evenings are too. In fact you have developed a habit of putting on your headlights irrespective of what time of day it is, as it seems to be permanently dark. One day the weather is windy. The next is bitterly cold. The following day it is wet to the proportions that you consider rekindling your Ark design company idea. And the next day is a mixture of the previous three days weather combined. Roll on summer.

Houston we have a problem; it's Safety November. Safety November should really just be called November as Safety has only a briefly passing relationship. Whatever Safety November wants to do it does, irrespective of what everyone would prefer it to do or what it would do in an ideal world. The rules are indeed made to be broken, and behaviour is as disengaged as possible. Like the disloyal house cat that disappears for days on end only to return for some warmth and food before popping back out on another sojourn, Safety November is hard to domesticate and train. As a Safety professional I have to manage this person carefully. Enforcement and standards are important for both the immediate Safety concerns of all as well as longer term issues of workforce engagement and overall culture. Equally, Safety November is the kind of person that has been routinely moved from one job to the next; a problem shared in this instance is not a problem halved, but one just moved to someone else. A "Not in My Back Yard" approach prevails frequently, but this approach is not one that actually solves the problem only to displace it.

The key issues with Safety November are ones of engagement and expectations. The final section of this book shall look at ways we can nudge Safety November somewhere a little warmer.

It's January. By the time January rolls around we have become used to the dark and dreary weather. We are also over fed and generally over indulged following the festive period. We have the added bonus of being 'invited' to shop in the sales to spend the remaining disposable income (or credit) that Christmas didn't vacuum up. The advertisements on the television are either of Internet dating sites or diet and exercise regimes. Wherein lays the dichotomy of January. January takes its name from the Roman god of the doorway, Janus, based on the Latin "Ianua," meaning door. January is two-faced; outwardly optimistic and filled with resolutions and aspirations, whilst deep down accepting that most of those won't last into February. Rather than symbolising real change and development it pays lip service to the notion whilst secretly acknowledging that actually nothing changes.

Two faced, cynical Safety January is a major problem for any industry. Outwardly Safety January can be optimistic for new initiatives, ideas and change whilst secretly preferring their failure and maintaining the status quo. Even more dangerously, they are keen to take other peoples New Year verve and aspirations and consume them into their cynical ambivalence. Such attitudes can prevail in all strata of an organisation, from workforce to board level. I have given presentations to executive boards and knew that looking back at me were many people with such an attitude. No organisation can change and achieve what I strongly believe 99% of the workforce would like to achieve if the prevailing hegemonic approach at the top is such. The attitude of Safety January needs to be identified and tackled at all levels. Far from being the start of a beautiful year, January shall extinguish many people's best intentions and aspirations before the month is out. I see it as one of my roles, as a Safety professional, to try help ensure that this doesn't happen and that people are protected from this attitude in order to fulfil their individual potential.

Using this model we can identify some key challenges for us regarding Health and Safety, especially when we look at making a difference and changing cultures. I am confident that most people that have taken the time and effort to buy and read this book would place themselves in the top left hand of the model; July.

So for all of us Safety July's we can see we have an important role to play in the challenges that lie ahead.

- To maintain our standards at all times and ensure complacency doesn't creep in.
- To identify people that have potential, make sure that they are supported and nurtured, and sheltered from adverse influences and attitudes.
- To challenge those not engaged. Not to compromise standards and expectations and to be creative in finding ways in which we can nudge them into a better place.
- To take the fight to those who resist change because we will not be able to make changes without addressing this. Ice ages may have seen the back of the dinosaurs, but they are painfully slow. We should be quicker to meet our goals.

And if you didn't consider yourself to be Safety July then my challenge is simple – what can you do to move in that direction?

So now we have an idea and framework we can place people's characteristics within, we need to move on with our analysis of Health and Safety. And if we want to make the difference and changes, then one group of people are surely very important in that goal?

Safety People

The Health and Safety professional has a poor reputation when viewed by the general public at large. At social engagements, or training courses I am delivering, I find myself having to quickly apply a pre-emptive strike in defence of my person as soon as the other people present find out that I am a Health and Safety professional. Before that moment, they may have thought I was a decent enough guy with reasonable social skills and an acceptable level of personal hygiene, but upon hearing that small facet of information their look and body language immediately changes as if I had just told them I had committed an unpleasant crime for which I had not received a custodial sentence.

It is reasonable to assume that given the whole profession of Health and Safety is tarnished to such a colossal extent then some of this is likely to be as a result of the people within the industry. Let me be very clear at this point; in no way am I saying every single person, but enough to create a stereotype and a stigma. If we want to change people, behaviours and cultures, we should spend at least a moment looking at ourselves.

Are there any more disliked professions than Health and Safety? Health and Safety professionals rank alongside other notorious roles, including policeman, traffic wardens, football referees or PE teachers. This is not just a problem with public relations or one that requires some clever marketing or branding exercise. There is a long term, historical stigma that has evolved around the Health and Safety professional.

With this notion in the back of my mind, I began to consider who on earth would choose to be a Health and Safety professional? There was a well documented piece written on precisely this subject in 1999 by Mike Buttolph in "Styles of Safety Practice." In this piece there were four categories identified which I have used as a start point for my analysis. I too have four categories of Safety practitioner, but have modified the names and some of the characteristics to fit my experience within the profession. Naturally there shall be some that do not fit neatly into one classification. I have written them deliberately broad and they are not meant to be considered a precise science, but more a rule of thumb. We shall now meet the four types of "Mr Health and Safety."

The Reverend:

Often the Rev came from the shop floor. The Rev may have been in, or around a serious accident, which shaped the more puritan nature that is displayed regarding Health and Safety. Whilst Safety is personal to the Rev, it may not always be communicated so that it can become personal to the person with whom the Rev is communicating or trying to influence, and the aloof detached manner in which they conduct themselves does not necessarily help in this goal. People that do not follow the Rev are wrong and are unable to understand the Revs' more enlightened viewpoint.

How does The Reverend ply his trade?

"Welcome this glorious Sunday morning my congregation and allow me to spend the following half an hour to eulogise about the importance of Health and Safety. I shall preach here from my lofty position within my pulpit and implore unto you to search your souls, at which point you will be able to confess your sins and follow me into the light." The Rev considers Health and Safety to be near sacred. The Rev also sees Safety as rather specialist. As a result, the rev acts detached from an organisation and sees Safety as very "top down."

Not long after I ventured away from the world of contracting and started my consultancy company I worked with a manufacturing company. Their Health and Safety manager was possibly not hugely pleased to have an external consultant popping in to provide additional support during a period in which the company was rapidly expanding, but we established a solid working relationship none the less. I was not party to the daily machinations of the organisation and merely acted as a pair of external eyes trying to ensure there wasn't anything missed during a time of such flux.

We'll call him 'Neville', the Safety manager, and he had worked for the company in one way, shape or form for over thirty years. During this time he had occupied many roles and felt he knew three things in the world more solidly than anybody else:

1) How the company operated
2) Health and Safety
3) Rochdale Football Club

It is also fair to note his knowledge on all three areas was particularly robust, and if all three areas of his personal curriculum were the subjects of a pub quiz he would win hands down.

They say that there is "none as zealous as the converted", and Neville had all the zeal of a converted soul. He admitted to having a healthy disregard for rules in his youth, although the rules were nowhere near as stringent during his youth, but sat down behind his desk wheezing from a chronic lung complaint brought on by a perfect mixture of things he inhaled during his working life as well as his social life. His dexterity was also not what it ought to be due to the exposure his hands had experienced to vibrating machinery. In one meeting we had to pause after he told me of the time someone had been killed in the factory and the effect it had had on him. When it came to Health and Safety, Nev the Rev, was a walking propaganda machine.

The experiences and knowledge the Neville had gained were considerable, but he tended to wield these powerful tools with the same precision my toddler grandson wields his spoon of carrot puree. He would energetically ask workers if they understood the difference between a WEL and a MEL. Or when identifying possible fire hazards would issue a quick spot test around HSE Guidance document 131 before returning to his office and slumping in his chair resigned to the fact that they "just didn't get it" and that it was a "good job he was there." Indeed it was, but his message of "be like me so you are not like me" was an odd paradox and one that readily muddied the Health and Safety water rather than make it clear and simple.

Sergeant Safety:

The Sergeant doesn't necessarily have been working within the police force or armed forces in a previous career. Anyone who has seen the classic British film Kes will remember the PE teacher whose egotistical and autocratic approach to managing people (whilst also comedic) is the perfect example of how Sergeant Safety can act in the real world.

How does Sergeant Safety ply his trade?

Sergeant Safety is enjoying a second career, possibly having previous been in gainful employment within the constabulary or having recently left a career serving the queen and country in her majesties armed forces. He or she is fantastic with rules and systems and now works as a Health and Safety officer. Not quite the same as weekend manoeuvres over the Brecon Beacons granted, but also generally less likely to get shot at.

There is no other way for the Sergeant to exist, but as a finely oiled cog in a machine of excellence, continually demanding the best of himself and those in his ranks. The paper work is as precise as his shirt is ironed. His army would be a much more effective unit if he could just back squad a couple of the inferior ones, but whilst the Sergeant possesses many virtues, a lifetime of "chain of command" highly autocratic leadership styles may not be compatible with the requirements of communication in the modern civilian world. A response of "because I said so", is to styles of communication as comparing the old rugby players diet of a pre-game 12 pints of beer with the modern high protein shakes and ice bath recoveries to the world of modern sport.

During the course of my career, I have encountered many Sergeant Safeties, but I remember meeting one a couple of years ago when working with a medium sized contractor, supporting their behavioural Safety initiative. The focus of my visit that particular day was to look at how we could improve the way in which Safety was communicated within the organisation and so I was to spend the day with their "Safety champion" who happened to be a very nice guy. So it was possibly not a total surprise that I had missed the gleaming stripes on the lapel of the Sergeant.

After a highly productive meeting a discussion about behavioural Safety more broadly, we decided to have a walk around the site continuing the discussion about the importance of placing a behavioural initiative within the business and the impact it should have. I still hadn't spotted the stripes.

Then, with the reactions of a Lion in the middle of the Serengeti the Sergeant broke off from our conversation making a sharp turn in direction of a young gazelle that had strayed too far from its mother's side. Actually, this 'gazelle' was a large and experienced Plant Operator. From about thirty yards away my college bellowed at the Plant Operator in a loud and aggressive tone to "get his ****ing seat belt on", before turning back to me to continue our discussion about the importance of engaging with the workforce when communicating Safety with a smile of satisfaction on his face.

The issue was not that this Sergeant was a bad bloke – far from it, he was a really nice guy. Nor was the issue with his career, or former career path. It was simply a view of how Health and Safety should operate and be communicated. He agreed with the ideas of behavioural Safety and understood the objective, but when it came to challenging long held ways of working, he came up short. Ultimately, rather than communicate in a manner befitting of the 21st century, the Sergeant just couldn't help, but shout at Casper to get off the crossbar.

The Official:

For more mature readers, 'Blakey' from On the Buses would fit the bill. Otherwise they are likely to have both paper and a clipboard, with an obstructive approach and a rule close at hand to justify it, irrespective of whether the rule is correct or being correctly applied.

How does The Official ply his trade?

The Official loves the rules. Whilst probably not from a practical background The Official is very well versed with the legislative requirements of Health and Safety. The Official likes to quote the rules chapter and verse. The authority that accompanies this role is central to The Official and the manner in which the work is undertaken. Problems are often found, deficiencies identified and scored on the inevitable clip board whilst solutions are left firmly in the domain of the workforce to rectify.

A classic example of The Official was when I worked for a multibillion pound contractor within the construction and civil engineering sphere. I was there to support the launch of a second phase of their behavioural program. I had been heavily involved with the first phase of the rollout of the behavioural initiative and despite overwhelming positive response from site managers and the workforce, a consistent item of feedback was offered.

"That's all great mate. If it happens then I am in. Has this message been given to the Safety team?"

This was a standard opening to a conversation. I would insist that yes indeed the Safety team had been part of the program and received the same message.

"Well they don't believe it. They are still *****", was a not untypical reply.

The issue was glaringly obvious. The site teams overwhelmingly supported the moral objective of the behavioural Safety journey, but the implementation of this was not helped by members of the Safety team insisting on reams of paperwork and ways in which they can score (or more accurately score down) the sites performance. This ran counter to the ethos of the initiative.

I was at a meeting with some key stakeholders and the subject came up. The Director of Health and Safety, who was a rather enlightened Safety professional, as well as being a decent guy, addressed the discrepancy between the moral importance of near miss reporting and the importance placed on the recording of these by certain parts of his Safety team. At one point he said something very close to the following:

"I would rather a guy did ten Safety discussions than two because he can only be bothered to write down two in some book. The idea is that we get to a point when no guy in this company has an issue with going to someone else and having

a chat about Safety. That is where we are trying to get to, but we have to migrate to there from this systems based approach we have currently."

Fairly progressive words you may feel. Dubious about the carrot of a utopian ideal being dangled in front of the thirty site managers in the room, one rather cynical and slightly angry man, aged in his mid-forties and whose entire body emitted a thousand signs that he had been in the construction game for many years longer chirped up.

"That's all great. Every bloke in here would agree with you. We will go and do tool box talks, do them the best we can and not worry too much about the signatures and all that paper like you just said."

As he spoke his fervour increased. His eyes turned to the Safety manager perched at the side of the room who was a fine mixture of confused, uninterested and bemused.

"But if we do all that, will you mark us down for not having tool box talks signed when you audit us next week?"

In front of the Director of Health and Safety for the entire plc, at the start of the launch of this phase of the program, and having just heard the visionary oratory of his director and commander and chief, he couldn't do anything, but acquiesce could he?

"Yes" he said solemnly. And in that moment the good will of thirty fine men, needed to make these changes everyone claimed they wanted to see was lost. Thirty years of prejudices reinforced. And one man excited at the thought of being able to score people down in the near future.

The Raggy Dolls:

Here lie the odds and sods. The randoms and the rejects. Here we find the person who is looking to come off the shop floor into something, well – safer. An individual without any grand desire or plan and just somehow end up in Safety. That is pretty much what happened to me. I would also like to point out that here also could lie a vast number of Safety professionals who spend part of their weekend as an amateur football referee, as well as a number of people who previously served with the armed forces and have altered their perspective and style and whilst still possess many of the qualities of their former colleague Sergeant Safety.

How do the Raggy Dolls ply their trade?

This random, rag tag bunch are the largest group by far in my experience. This book is largely, although in no uncertain terms exclusively, an appeal to people who would fit within this group.

Have you ever been exasperated by stories of 'Elf and Safety' in the national press? Or found yourself defending the profession again absurd cases such as 'Conkers Bonkers' or someone who is incredulous at your profession? Do you find yourself thinking that there was proof if ever it was needed that 'Health and Safety has gone mad'? Do you ever think it is probably down to meddling from Brussels? In that case I am hoping to find a resonating chord within this book.

Or have you been at a meeting where Sergeant Safety guffaws at the suggestion that a more holistic approach to Safety should be implemented as 'booky bollocks' as I have, instantly dismissing any notion of different approaches in communication as 'not being in the real world' and think Steven Spielberg missed a trick when casting for Jurassic Park?

Have you been confused when a member of the Safety department, like The Official, tells gleefully how he managed to score down a site on a recent audit as they had managed to omit to put their weekly scaffold checks, which were fully present, correct and up to date, but in the wrong part of the file, "he put them in section 6 and not section 7. I showed him. You should have seen his face!"

Have you ever looked around, wondered how on earth you ended up doing this, despair with some of your colleagues and peers and think – if only everyone just did it right, for the right reason and in the right way – we could make a real difference and not be vilified in the process?

Behavioural Safety

Some reading this book will be fully conversant with the ideas of Behavioural Safety. They may well have a behavioural programme within their organisation and attended various training workshops. There may be some poor souls that have attended one of mine. Equally there may well be vast numbers of people to whom the concept of Behavioural Safety is a total mystery. It is not my plan to write another Behavioural Safety textbook in the traditional way, or to plagiarise existing work. However, a brief over view of what the behavioural approach to Safety is and why it exists will be helpful for us to plot some of the dots of Health and Safety in the future.

Historically, Health and Safety has been approached with a significant emphasis on fulfilling legal responsibilities. Most management systems were established to ensure compliance with the Health and Safety at Work etc Act, 1974. This is an entirely correct thing to do. Being legally compliant with the Act as well as the raft of subsequent regulation should help provide a safer working environment for employees.

I still encounter some organisations whose almost sole motivation is to achieve legal compliance in terms of Safety. I say this with a somewhat negative tone because I believe such an approach is flawed and can create problems that run counter to our goal. A management approach solely based on legal compliance focuses on the concept of mitigation. This means that should the organisation be brought to court they will be able to prove their compliance with the rules and mitigate their liability. It is the classic "cover your arse" approach, which still reverberates around industry.

The problem with this approach is that it implicitly accepts the fact that accidents happen as long as the company or individuals are not fined or imprisoned. This overlooks the fact an individual has been unfortunate enough to suffer some sort of loss or injury. The morality of the system is lost.

Irrespective of the balance between legal motivations and moral ones, any company would have to ensure legal compliance. As a result, as the company grows it would be expected that a greater amount of resources be ploughed into Health and Safety. This is seen all around us with the audits, routine training, risk assessments, method statements and inductions. Safety bureaucracy that we all know and love.

Much of this is necessary and required by law. Unfortunately most systems I have seen become bloated, duplicated and sometimes misapplied along the way. Crucially, we would also expect that during this period of growth, the companies' Safety performance improves and matures.

Once an organisation has developed cultural maturity, a robust management system and structured embedded procedures we come to a crucial juncture. People think "what more can we do?" Despite vast swathes of paper, training matrices and memorandums, we still find a residual level of accidents. People still get hurt. Employees die after having gotten out of bed in the morning to go to work.

It is at this point where behaviours become more important. Behavioural approaches cannot succeed without a sensible, compliant and healthy system of Safety management, but can work within a system to significantly improve performance. Accidents that I have investigated focus on what the people did, rather than whether the piece of paper was signed. Safety is about people. Ultimately accidents are more dependent upon the decisions that people make, i.e. their behaviour.

As a result this book is focussed on the human condition, the frailty of our minds. How can we can use this understanding to reduce the likelihood of that person whose alarm went at 5am and took their lunch out of their fridge to go to work only to never return? The research for this book did not centre on the traditional behavioural Safety tomes which some of you may well be familiar with, but on the concept of decision making in other areas of science.

During his acceptance speech for the Nobel Prize for economics in 2002, Vernon Smith, said

"I urge students to read narrowly within economics, but widely in science. Within economics there is essentially only one model.... the economic literature is not the best place to find new inspiration beyond these traditional technical models of modelling."

It is this principal I have adopted when researching and writing this book. There is relatively little novel research within behavioural Safety. The ideas within this field have remained constant for years, whilst other areas have accelerated their understanding of how humans make decisions. This has provided a wealth of knowledge that could be applied to Safety in order to improve performance within this area. In doing so we may also be able to close the gap between the goals of behavioural Safety and their achievement.

Before we can try to close this gap, we need to visit, or revisit, the established norms of behavioural Safety.

How behaviour affects Safety

Put very simply behaviour is the things that people do, and the way in which they do them. Whilst we are all unique and have an array of personal indulgences the way in which our brain has evolved is common to us all. As a result we are all more likely to act in a certain way, and make certain decisions if a set of environmental triggers are in place. This is crucial when considering Health and Safety.

If we were to delve a little deeper into this concept we would find that when left to their own devices people are likely display the following behaviour:

1. Do what interests or motivates us as individuals.
2. Do just enough to get by and take personal risks.
3. Cut corners.

We shall now look at these factors with greater detail.

1. Do what interests or motivates us as individuals

If I ask a group of delegates or workers what motivates them, what do you think is the number one answer a vast majority of the time? Yes, you guessed right: Money.

In the period of austerity, money is in the forefront of people's minds to an even greater extent. There is constant pressure for efficiency and the costs of jobs are driven down. There are significant numbers of people, working directly for companies and those that form part of a supply chain, who have less job security. It would be churlish to dismiss this factor when considering people's behaviour at work. There is little point in discussing a notional Health and Safety initiative that doesn't bare any resemblance to what actually occurs in people's lives. The truth is that money is important. It forms a huge part of the working psyche.

I encounter many people who virtuously say that they don't think money should come in to Health and Safety decisions, but if we examine people and the actions they take, their mind set at that given time and their key drivers, money is often first and foremost in their minds. So the real question is why?

Jason is a twenty four year old construction worker. He dislikes everything to do with Health and Safety. He dislikes and doesn't respect the site Safety officer and has many colourful names for him. All he wants to do is his job and go home.

This is not an unusual set of circumstances. If we analyse Jason a little more deeply and consider his motivations we would understand that the reason he dislikes the 'over-the-top rules' is because he wants to earn as much money as possible. And why is this so important to him? It is important because he has a young wife and daughter at home. He wants to give them both all he can. The challenge for Jason is to make that link between cause and effect. The money is for his family and aspirant lifestyle, neither of which is possible if he is off work due to an incident or worse. So if Jason, in the style of Cuba Gooding Junior in Jerry Maguire wants you to "show him the money" ask him "Why? What for?"

2. Doing just enough to get by and taking personal risks

It is a dark and dreary November evening. After spending the last few hours sitting in a large grey box on a long grey road under a dark grey sky I have returned home, and after a brief chat with my loving wife of over thirty years (please note I put in that sentence voluntarily and not due to external pressure) I assume my position in my favourite chair and reach for the remote control. Within seconds, and without much conscious thought, Sky Sports appears in front of me. Soon enough I am engrossed in the live football spectacular from League One. And then, on the stroke of half time, the bulb in the 'big light' blows and the dog goes mad. At this point I am presented with a decision to make.

I could sit in the darkness and enjoy the cinematic effect that that provides, but I know that that merely delays the problem. And possibly increases the likelihood of the hazard that has not yet realised actually realising. Currently that hazard is sitting in the room next door watching Coronation Street in a state of relative contentment. Finding me sitting in the dark may change her serene emotional state. I opt to not sit in the dark.

Given that I am somewhat vertically challenged, the task of changing the light bulb is more labour intensive for me than it would be for others that are taller than five feet eight inches. So given that I can't reach the now useless light bulb, I require assistance. My wife is shorter still and so of no use. Added to that, if I disturb her whilst she is watching the events unfold in Weatherfield that particular hazard is likely to be realised.

I know that my step ladders are in the shed at the bottom of the garden. I could go down the garden, trudge through the long, wet grass to the shed and then fight my way over the barbecue that still sits forlornly after another glorious British summer before wrestling my trusty step ladder back down the garden with me to the house. On entering the house I would have to be careful to not tread my muddy trainers into the carpet before changing the light bulb. And then I would have to return my step ladder over the soggy lawn until it finally rests snugly back behind my old set of golf clubs and the sledge that appeared sometime around 1993. All this to achieve in sufficiently short a time to rush back to my favoured position for the second half of Yeovil versus Stevenage.

Alternatively, I could just pop into the dining room and take the nearest chair back to the offending light before deftly jumping up to change the bulbs over before returning the chair to the dining room and myself to my chair, probably via the fridge for a suitable second half beverage.

Which option do you think I take? Which option do you think a vast majority of people would take?

Of course I take the dining room chair option, as would most people, but why? I am an experienced Health and Safety professional. I address working at height issues permanently. I know that the safest and correct thing to do would be to use the stepladder. I have one for such a task sitting ready. I am competent, knowledgeable and experienced. Yet I still choose the chair.

This is because we all, to varying extents, have the 'lazy gene' and will do just enough to get by. I know the correct thing to do, but I shall assess the risks and if I perceive that the risk to me is suitably low or at an acceptable level I shall take that risk on, irrespective of the rules or what is correct.

When I have been asked to investigate an incident, the individual involved more often than not knew precisely the systems that should have been followed and had received the appropriate level of training. That individual decided to ignore all that advice and knowledge and changed their behaviour to an alternative pattern. Quite often it is a direct result of people's innate tendency to want to do 'just enough to get by.' This partly explains why organisations' Safety performance plateaus around level three of the Organisational Maturity model and that despite all the systems being in place and enforced, people will still choose to deviate from them and behave in a different way resulting in an accident or incident.

3. Cut corners.

The final key area of people's behaviour is their propensity to cut corners. You only have to walk around a newly built housing estate and see lines worn in the recently laid grass where people have slowly-but-surely begun to tread a new path. They divert from the pathways designed and laid especially for their journeys to and fro. These new paths are known as 'desire lines', but what do these lines tell us about people's behaviour?

The instinctive and obvious answer is that these new paths are quicker. This is of course perfectly true, but how much time do these short cuts save us? Normally seconds at most, so what material difference do those few seconds actually make? And yet our brains are programmed to seek these seconds out and offer us a small psychological 'wins'.

This small facet of human psyche provides us with a few insights regarding Health and Safety. Firstly it demonstrates a person's inbuilt desire to hunt down seconds and save them. Some people suggest to me that this behaviour is healthy as it promotes efficiency and progress. Sometimes that is true, but it may increase the risk within a task or place someone in greater potential danger.

The importance of a belief

There is a secondary totem pole that stands adjacent to the one for behaviour. It is belief. Beliefs are very important when initiating behavioural Safety initiatives and trying to positively impact on an organisations Safety culture. So why is a belief so integral to changing people's behaviours regarding Health and Safety?

Working with various clients over the years, I have had this discussion with countless directors and managers. I have explained countless times why behavioural Safety starts with having the correct beliefs in place. There are also many other 'belief based behavioural Safety' initiatives. Indeed 'belief based leadership' is a well documented area which I shall not digress into at this juncture. So allow me to have the same conversation with your good self now. Why does changing Safety behaviours start with a belief?

A belief is a strongly held conviction, something that an individual holds to be true. The belief can be of any persuasion, it can be a positive belief about Safety or a negative belief. It could also be somewhere in between. Our

Safety leaders, the people that wish the Health and Safety year to be July, will be far more likely to be in possession of positive Safety beliefs than people who live in the more adversarial month of January. For example, a positive Safety belief may be that "Safety is more important than productivity"; the more negative version being that productivity is more paramount than Safety. This can occur when commercial pressures of deadlines become an increasingly prominent factor in the work being undertaken.

People's attitudes will be directly linked to the beliefs that they possess. Consequently, my Safety leader who believes that Safety is more important than productivity will know that the rules are important and adhere to them. This is in sharp contrast to the individual who possesses the opposing belief, who thinks it is acceptable to break rules from time to time if the programme or demands of the job dictate it to be necessary to cut the occasional corner. After all, as long as the job is done it is not so important exactly how it is achieved, because that individual believes that it is the productivity, and not the Safety, that is more important.

It is people's attitudes which will shape their expectations of work and how Safety is, or ought to be, managed. The July based Safety leader believes the rules to be important and so expects them to be enforced consistently and fairly. They will reinforce their belief of the primacy of Safety over production. Their January based foe will learn and expect people to turn a blind eye or not enforce the rules rigidly to allow the individual to complete their task. These individuals are fulfilling their belief in the primacy of production.

The consequences of these processes are obvious. The Safety leader, in possession of the positive Safety belief, shall display good Safety based behaviours, whereas the person with the negative belief will display poor Safety behaviours.

There you have a quick whistle stop tour, explaining why beliefs are important when trying to change people's Safety behaviours and an organisations Safety culture. I have never worked with an organisation or project where a world class Safety performance and a positive Safety culture existed without people at a senior level sharing the deeply held conviction that Safety is of ultimate importance. How can an organisation become world class at anything unless they believe that they can do so?

Mohammed Ali was once asked when he knew he would be "the greatest." This is how he replied;

"I would have been the world's greatest at whatever I did. If I were a garbage man, I'd be the world's greatest garbage man! I'd pick up more garbage and faster than anyone has ever seen. To tell you the truth, I would have been the greatest at whatever I'd done!"

Ali knew that success started with belief. If we are going to try to genuinely improve things and change Health and Safety away from the cheap punch line it has become, it is crucial to believe that it should happen, that it could happen and it will happen.

Conscious and unconscious thoughts

One of the key ideas within behavioural Safety and achieving a 'just culture' is the distinction between an error and a violation. Simply put an error is a mistake. An error occurs due to a subconscious action or decision, which results in an unintended outcome. They occur as a result our own human frailty; our imperfections. It is this frailty that gives rise to the perception of 'accidents happen mate – we aren't robots.' It is true that people are not robots. No one expects people to perform as such. However, a robust Health and Safety system should have sufficient precautions in place to take into account these imperfections and stop harm from actualising.

A violation is different. A violation is a deliberate, conscious act in which a person deviates from a known system or breaks a rule. There has been a lot of academic work analysing violations, and they can be categorised into sub levels. These are routine violations, exceptional violations, situational violations and optimising violations. For ardent Safety academics these distinctions are important, but in the realms of the real world they have little value. It is the aim of this book to look at these rule breaks and what we can do to challenge them, promote a better Safety culture and positively impact on Safety performance.

If a person perceives a rule or procedure to be bad, or overly inefficient this increases the likelihood that they will seek to deviate from it, to seek out those extra seconds, to find that psychological 'win', and in short violate procedure. This would be considered an 'optimising violation'. Violations of this type suggest areas in which procedures could be improved or perceived too onerous, but may also lead to unsafe behaviour. If "The Official" insists on a dynamic risk assessment to be conducted for every activity, even handing over a set of keys (as one facilities manager bemoaned to me recently), all The Official achieves is disenfranchising and disengaging the workforce, increasing the likelihood for people to violate and perpetuate a poor Safety culture.

Ideally, our Safety systems would, where possible, lay along mental 'desire lines' making it more likely for people to follow the correct path and not plough their own potentially less safe path. This would decrease the desire of individuals to cut corners and violate.

The distinction between the unconscious thought processes involved with an error is in sharp contrast to the conscious thought process of the violations. It is this distinction that is central to the theory that all accidents are preventable.

If I ever ask a group whether they think that all accidents are preventable I get an array of responses. Anything and everything from disillusionment and incredulity, through to just plain swearing. Unsurprisingly, most responses are of the negative variety. People are not perfect, so accidents happen. The reason why this theory exists is that in accident causation analysis people are allowed to be imperfect, make mistakes or commit errors. Because these are unconscious acts it is difficult or near impossible to prevent them. People are not perfect.

However, the analysis always finds violations. Violations are the result of a conscious thought process, and therefore they should be challenged and changed. The theory that all accidents are preventable is a result of this distinction. A Safety system should be able to compensate for human error. We are not expected to be perfect and as long as people do not deviate from the rules or procedures then the accident will not come into realisation. Accidents are preventable.

So far, so good?

That's good, because in the next section I shall commit Health and Safety blasphemy and challenge this theory which has become central to Health and Safety convention. I shall then look at what we can do to achieve our goals of improving Safety performance. How can we bring about a beautiful, sunny and lasting Safety July?

66

Section Two:

The flaw in the theory and what we can do about it

The elephant in the room

In Mark Twain's story The Stolen White Elephant, the activities of the rather inept detectives are detailed as they search for an aforementioned elephant that was right on the spot after all. Since then the phrase has become synonymous with any issue that is blaringly obvious, but nobody seems is willing to mention or discuss.

At the end of the last section, I outlined the theory that all accidents are preventable. The justification for this being the different classification of conscious and unconscious actions, the violations and the errors, whereby Safety management systems should be able to compensate for human error and provided that we follow the rules and do not choose to consciously violate then the accident will be prevented. In classic Health and Safety training, this is often referred to as the Swiss Cheese model where all the holes line up in a straight line to allow realisation and only one of those holes needs to shift for the accident to not occur. Remove the violations and the holes will never line up, even with errors occurring.

It is a theory that is not as complex to understand as some, like String Theory or the Theory of Relativity. It is simple, elegant and offers us Safety professionals with a tantalising glimpse of the Safety utopia to which we would hope to achieve. It also has helped elevate thinking with Health and Safety and further behavioural approaches and I confess to being both excited and impressed when coming across it.

I do not wish to shoot this theory down in flames or suggest it has no relevance or place within Health and Safety. However, I felt that there was a problem with it almost a second after the brief and rather tragic sensation of excitement upon first hearing it. Unbeknown to be at that time it was the elephant in the room.

I am not the only person to come across the elephant. Most people to whom I explain the reason why all accidents are preventable experience the elephant. The chances are that you may well have during your reading of the last section.

I have spent hours on courses dissecting errors and violations, exploring case studies and real life examples to finally reach a glorious crescendo justifying why all accidents are preventable. I look expectantly at the audience hoping for some grand conversion like Paul on the road to Damascus, only to see faces less hostile to the concept than before, but still not entirely convinced. I do not put this lack of conviction down to a lack of clarity, coherence or interest, but instead it is a result of the elephant in the room.

I may well be an old cynic these days, but when something looks and sounds too good to be true then I have a feeling in my stomach that it probably is too good to be true. Granted, the sensation may well be the slight over indulgence in my local pub the night before, but I like to think it is the experience garnered over the years. Similarly to my not entirely convinced cohorts my theory doesn't quite fit into what we recognise as the real world. In the theoretical or academic world it may be elegant, but accidents happen in the real world, and that certainly isn't ideal.

It was this feeling, along with my quest to delve deeper into the human condition that took me far from the beaten path of Safety academia. I have delved deeper in order to examine this a little further and apply my learning to the world of Health and Safety.

What do you mean 'rational'?

Safety at the behavioural level focuses on decision making. There are two main fields within academia that study decision making and its consequences. These are psychology and economics. In recent years these two fields have merged in some areas and consequently the research in 'behavioural economics' is often also cited within 'behavioural psychology.' It is with little surprise that I migrated from the world of Safety and started my search for greater understanding in this area. Bare with me a little here as we are about to deviate considerably from the well trodden path of Safety books of yore.

It was interesting to me during this process that the two main strands of psychology and economics, which I felt most applicable to Health and Safety, both started with a key distinction used in a different way. Throughout the rest of the book we shall explore these two strands in more detail as well as their application to behavioural Safety, but first I think it beneficial to analyse this key distinction more fully.

Normally when we consider the subject of Economics we think about business and money. However, in reality it is more closely concerned with peoples' decisions and behaviour; "if the price of butter increases what happens to peoples' choices?" "How many people would decide to invest if the interest rate rose by 5%?" So the behaviour of people and the decisions they are likely to make is a key part of economics then it may be of potential value and interest to us in Safety.

When considering these choices, the people or 'agents' to use economic parlance, are considered to be 'rational.' The agent is seen as 'rational' in the sense that well-being as defined by utility (which is economic speak for the amount of satisfaction someone gets from using or consuming something) is optimized given perceived opportunities. That is, the agent seeks to attain very specific and predetermined goals to the greatest extent with the least possible cost. The rational agent always makes the best choice for themselves.

Already this will probably create some alarm bell in the head when considering the real world. The rational agent is also assumed to be in possession of certain things, namely:

- The decision being made is clear
- The agent can identify all possible alternatives available
- That the alternatives can be ranked and weighed
- The preferences of the rational agent are constant over time
- The agent possesses perfect information about the market in question
- The agent shall choose the option which is best

I think most readers would agree, that is quite a shopping list of assumptions, even if some of the economic language isn't too user friendly. However, this principle runs through the entirety of economic orthodoxy and so theories about what decisions people will make are based on the person being an 'economically rational agent,' despite the above list bearing little or no resemblance to any decision making situation in the real world.

Some economists suggest that the idea of the 'rational agent' was based on assumptions that were fit for the 19th century. In this era modern economics was emerging as an academic pursuit, which begs the question "how is it sensible to use an approach to decision making which is based on an era of the telegram in the era of the internet?" How is it fit for purpose, sensible and is it the best we can offer?

It may be worth at this point reflecting on my issue with Health and Safety approaches being forty years out of date when some economic principles can more than triple that and in comparison Safety is positively up to date.

This now leads me to the main critique with the theory that all accidents are preventable. The distinctions of conscious and unconscious thought are valid and useful; however, the leap to the conclusion above is based upon the supposition of a "rational agent". This theory has a set of assumptions that are centuries out of date. That was the intuitive white elephant in the room that most of us sense when considering this theory. In theory it works. In reality it is flawed. And it is flawed as a result of the assumption of the rational agent.

Before we continue down this road further, I fell that it may be prudent to look in more detail at the rational economic man. A reasonably typical example of the rational agent in action would be when considering whether to buy Coca-Cola or

Pepsi. Normally the agent would prefer to consume Coca-Cola. However if the price of Coca-Cola was to increase by 5% then the option of consuming Pepsi instead would become more attractive. A 'rational agent' would definitely buy the Pepsi, whereas an 'irrational agent' would decide to buy the Coca-Cola anyway because he prefers the taste. In economic language this is "deriving greater utility."

Another example would be the decision to buy Marmite. Marmite has itself become part of the British lexicon for something that is extremely polarising and indeed is clearly demonstrated at my house. My wife loves the stuff and I can't stand it. Ordinarily I would never contemplate purchasing Marmite and I certainly would not consider eating it. With that said, there could be a price change that would cause me to change my mind. I think it would probably need to be -£50 before I would consider eating it, after which I would immediately wash my mouth out with plenty of Tetley's. This all fits within the theory of economical rational behaviour.

The examples offered above are relatively simple decisions and choices, but in the 21st century such decisions are few and far between. The range of choices that are available to us, and the amount of information about those choices, has expanded exponentially. This has occurred since the development of the idea of economic rationality. When buying electronic goods such as a new television, or acquiring a new mobile phone, how easy is it to be entirely confident we have made the optimal choice for us? Do we always act as 'rational agents?' Or do we have a best guess, a hunch and quietly say to ourselves "that'll do?"

We have begun to discuss the white elephant in the corner. The problem with the theory that all accidents are preventable is that it assumes a level of rationality based on a model that is not fit for the modern world. We do not all act as 'rational agents' 100% of the time. Like classical economic models that rely on a presumption of 'economic rationality' that do not fit perfectly the real world because humans do not always make rational decisions. Our current application of behavioural Safety also relies on such rationality. A rationality that simply does not exist; our decision making now is too complex, with a vast array of information not to mention a huge amount of time related pressure. Conscious thoughts and the psychology of violations are more complex than the polar, simplistic painting outlined earlier. So, if we are to change culture and improve Safety performance we shall have to delve a little deeper still.

How much of an island are we on?

There is another issue with the idea of rational behaviour. The rational agent makes decisions irrespective of those around them. Each man is an island, as they say. This is an assumption that not only does not fit with the modern world, but sits diametrically opposed to the ideas of behavioural Safety.

We are interested in helping change the culture of Health and Safety, to make it more like July in our Model of the Year. We considered in the first section just how far we have to travel as a profession. Cultures and fashions have both similarities and differences. A fashion will come and go whereas cultures exert changes gradually over time.

The theory of economic rationality does not offer an explanation for fashions and trends. Why do some things become popular to a greater extent than can be justified by optimal decision making by individuals? This is because of the social nature of humans, the way we interact, our attitudes, personalities, competition and awareness of our neighbour's decisions. As technology pushes the social envelope even further this effect becomes more pronounced. Although with that said I still can't understand why my Son is attached to Facebook and Twitter, or why he seems determined that I should learn to 'tweet'.

This is explained by something called Network Theory. Network Theory examines the links between people and how individual decisions can be effected by those of another. It is particularly insightful when considering how to change cultures. Although I should point out that the networks used here are not necessarily those related to the Internet and multimedia. Network effects can be witnessed throughout history. It is the immediacy and availability of their use that has been multiplied by the advent of modern technology.

There has been a very effective experiment which has demonstrated the impact that a neighbours decision can have on us, even when we consider ourselves to be autonomous and independent. Three scientists; Duncan Watt, Peter Dodds and Matt Salganik, created an artificial music market with over 14,000 teenage participants.

On arrival, the participants were split into two groups and each individual asked to download tracks of their choosing from a database of forty-eight. Each group was provided different information when deciding to download a track. The first group were given the name of the song and band then listened to a section of the track and forced to rate them between zero and five, before having the option to download. This mirrors the world of economic rational behaviour. The results showed that for this group there was a difference in popularity between the tracks, as would be expected. The most popular track was three times more popular than the least popular track.

The second group were given the identical task, however they were all able to see how many times each track had been downloaded previously. This time there was a marked difference in decision making. The two most popular tracks dwarfed the others available, and compared to the least popular was downloaded not to a ratio of 3:1, but over 30:1.

There was another very interesting result within this experiment. Surprisingly, the most popular tracks of the two groups were different. Knowing which song is fashionable not only effects how many downloads each track received, but also which song was likely to become most popular. This experiment was repeated on several occasions and the same track did not consistently come out as number one. Seemingly any track could easily become wildly popular or have next to zero downloads as a result of the behaviour of other people within a group.

This reinforces the fact that being dependent upon economically rational behaviour will not provide us with the decision making we would hope or expect as it fails to take into account the impact that other people have on our decision making. The simplistic analysis of conscious and unconscious thoughts is not sufficient to prevent accidents. Even when someone is acting consciously and considers themselves to be making an optimal decision, the reality is that there are other factors that influence our behaviour. So, if the current use of the idea of rationality when considering human behaviour is insufficient; where do we go from here?

Noel, Isaac, John and Herb

During the 1990's I had the dubious fortune of raising two teenagers. A joy of which some of you shall be able to empathise with I am sure. During this period my son became the body incarnate of his Britpop hero Noel Gallagher. He spent hours sulkily strumming away to Wonderwall in his bedroom. I became indoctrinated by proxy to Oasis and their catalogue of hits. Following their heyday they released a succession of albums to considerably less acclaim. Not that this stopped my son from purchasing said albums, including their 2000 release, 'Standing on the Shoulder of Giants'. According to my son, Mr Gallagher Senior (the more articulate and evolved edition in contrast to his more Neanderthal-like younger brother) miswrote a quote that he heard and liked when in a pub. The misquote became the album title.

The misquote was meant to read "standing on the shoulders of giants." This (more famous) original was written by one of the greatest ever physicists Sir Isaac Newton. In the age of enlightenment there were many great minds discovering new aspects of science. Isaac Newton's great rival was Robert Hooke, who has been described as the English Leonardo, such was the scope and breadth of his work. In January 1672, Newton was elected to the Royal Society, a loose organization of scientists and intellectuals. Shortly thereafter, he presented a paper detailing his discoveries in optics, and developed his rivalry with Robert Hooke, who harshly criticized Newton's research. This rivalry would percolate throughout the 1670s as Newton continued to work through the mathematics of gravity. This rivalry continued until the mid 1680s at which point Newton finally published his work, some of which Hooke felt had been stolen from him. Newton's research was organized into a three-volume book, the *Philosophiae Naturalis Principia Mathematica* ('Mathematical Principles of Natural Philosophy'), known to posterity as the *Principia*. It set forth Newton's three laws of motion, and proceeded to set forth the theory of gravitation, and back it up with rigorous mathematical proofs. Although the theory had many detractors at first, the scientific community would ultimately embrace it, and the Newtonian world-view would dominate physics until the 20th century.

The two men were no doubt brilliant and both desperately searching for the same things. In response to Hooke's criticism, Newton wrote to him. His letter famously said;

"What Des-Cartes did was a good step. You have added much several ways, and especially in taking ye colours of thin plates into philosophical consideration. If I have seen further it is by standing on ye shoulders of Giants."

In part this was a slight at Hooke's less than considerable stature. It was also an unabashed claim that his vision was true, perfect and beyond critique. It could easily be suggested that Newton demonstrated considerable hubris, especially given his rivals intellectual gravitas.

The reason for these two stories is to allow me to place myself and this book in perspective. I do not consider myself to be a pioneer such as Newton, but compare myself instead to a magpie like Gallagher. Noel Gallagher has often been cited for using his inspirations within his work. They included Bolan, Lennon and McCartney and Weller to name a few. My inspirations and research for this project are all identified either within the text or Further Reading section at the end of the book. And it is with this methodology in mind that I shall now turn to two more luminaries. They may not be as famous as the afore mentioned individuals, but are equally as useful in our consideration of the idea of rationality and human behaviour.

John Maynard Keynes is the more famous of the two protagonists. Keynes is one of the most famous economists of the last century and achieved a storied career. The piece of work he is most recognised for is "The General Theory of Employment, Interest and Money", often just referred to as "The General Theory." This was published in 1936 and used as a foundation of most post-war economic thinking. In the quarterly 'Journal of Economics,' Keynes wrote an article to clarify parts of the "General Theory." Within this, he was the first to question the idea of the rational economic agent. He proceeded to offer some thoughts on the matter.

"Knowing that our individual judgment is worthless, we endeavour to fall back on the judgment of the rest of the world which is perhaps better informed. That is, we endeavour to conform with the behaviour of the majority or average. The psychology of a society of individuals each of whom is endeavouring to copy the others leads to what we may strictly call a conventional judgment."

Here Keynes argues a revised idea of rationality which takes into account what people are more likely to do, especially when decisions are difficult, complex or pressured. Within this passage, Keynes anticipates the idea of networks and how other people affect decision making by decades.

The final member of my behavioural quartet is the most obscure. He would probably be the one playing bass in the band. His name is Herbert "Herb" Simon. Herb was an American born economist and is considered to be the godfather of behavioural economics, with much of his work focussing on decision making. Many of the people we shall stumble across in the final section are disciples of Herb Simon's work, although it should be noted that mainstream economics has not yet embraced the key messages of his work from the 1950's.

His main focus of work was to challenge the concept of economic rationality so that it bore a closer likeness to how agents actually behaved (whether that agent is an individual or a company). In 1955, in the same Quarterly Journal of Economics that Keynes had written in eighteen years earlier, Herb wrote;

"Traditional economic theory postulates an 'economic man' who, in course of being 'economic' is also 'rational' ... Recent

developments in economics, and in particular in the theory of the business firm, have raised doubts as to whether this schematized model of economic man provides a suitable foundation on which to erect a theory. ... The task is to replace global rationality of economic man with a kind of rational behaviour which is compatible with the access to information and computational capacities that are actually possessed by organisms, including man, in the kinds of environments in which such organisms exist."

The last section shall pay closer consideration to the 'computational capacities' and how that can affect behaviour. For now, we shall consider how can the ideas of Keynes, Simon and those that followed be used to help us in our quest to improve Health and Safety?

Achieving cultural change

John Maynard Keynes said that when decisions are difficult or complex, people will *"endeavour to conform with the behaviour of the majority or average."* The music download experiment of Watt, Dodds and Salganik demonstrated the power other people's decisions can have. When looking to raise Safety performance and overcome the limitations of individual rationality (in the economic, rather than broader sense), it is imperative that we consider the power of these inherent networks and the importance of establishing the correct culture.

Attempting to achieve a significant and radical cultural change within an organisation or industry can seem overwhelming. A self perpetuating belief of its impossibility is easily generated, especially on the backdrop of previously failed promises of change for the better. In this section I want to scour a variety of theories to see if we can find a more reliable and successful route towards our Health and Safety utopia.

Whenever I encounter someone who is convinced that change is impossible, where the prevailing Safety hegemony is enshrined in granite, I tend to offer one simple example. If we were to transport back in time to 2006 and tell someone that they were forbidden from smoking in public places, there would probably be a strong response. The fashionable and super skinny in Los Angeles may embrace such a folly, but the sensible British never would agree to such folly. Roll forward a few years and look what has happened. Compliance with the smoking ban has become normality. Not only that, but our attitudes and behaviour have changed as well. There is a man who drinks in my local pub, who following a heart attack a couple of years ago tried to quit smoking. As part of this, like many others across the country, he drags on an imitation cigarette to accompany his pint. No matter how many times it happens, and despite the fact that I know what he is doing, whenever I catch him dragging on his 'cigarette' I swiftly execute a double take of disbelief. In my mind I automatically react. "That's not the way we do things around here". In short, culture has changed significantly. Achieving cultural change is not impossible.

To effectively change culture, without the resources and help of the British legal system, the interactions between individual's decisions and actions are paramount. The key to success lies in the revised sense of rationality outlined by John Maynard Keynes, where people choose to conform to the majority. More simply speaking, this describes the use of networks.

There are many different types of network; however these can be reduced to three broad "signatures" based on the work by both Herb Simon and latterly Paul Ormerod. We shall now look at these three types of network and how they work before furthering our discussion on changing culture.

The first network to consider is the 'random network'. As its name implies the main feature of a random network is that it does not have structure. We may not immediately consider that our behaviour could be affected by people with whom we have no knowledge or direct interaction, but it is possible. Within the vicinity of my house there are probably eight or nine pubs, the nearest one of which is my local. The second nearest one used to be quite busy and so on occasion would pop in for a cheeky drink, but a couple of years ago it changed management and the pub suddenly emptied. What happened to my behaviour? I stopped going in also, perpetuating the emptiness of the pub. The choices of random strangers made me defer to their behaviour, exactly as

Keynes discussed. Another example would be how infectious diseases are spread. Someone with the flu could pass those germs onto someone entirely at random who in turn would do the same. There is no link between the people, but changes occur irrespectively.

The second network is called a 'scale free network'. In a scale free network there are a number of hubs, at the centre of which are key influencers. These influencers each have a number of links to individuals which they can influence. One of the main characteristics of the 'scale free network' is that the influencers can be anybody within a structure. It is not dependent on official levels of power. Instead, the number of links the influencer has with individuals that can be influenced is the important aspect.

To complete the trilogy, the third network is a 'small world network'. These are similar to 'scale free networks' in many ways however there are no hubs of influencers. This is a network of friends of friends. One person influences their friend who in turn influences another friend. The first person can influence a lot of people despite having no direct contact with them.

I anticipate that the second network was the one that had most immediate resonance with you in terms of application to Safety at work. It is the use of this type of network that we shall return to.

Before we do that, I started this section by acknowledging that changing culture was possible, if recognised to be difficult. I would like to take a short detour to study someone who has a vast track record of achieving precisely our goal. We may also find some network effects in the process.

Bill Bratten: Super-cop

Through the 1980's and first half of the 1990's New York had become one of the most dangerous cities within the United States of America. In fact, crime had become so rife that the press referred to the Big Apple as the Rotten Apple. The culture within the police was simply to react to crimes once they were committed, rather than trying to prevent them from occurring. It was simply "the way they did things around here." The workforce, numbering 35,000 also had cultivated a reputation for being a group that were hard to manage.

This was the rather depressing and murky picture that presented itself to one William Bratten in February 1994 when he was appointed police commissioner of New York City. Within two years, Bill Bratten turned New York into the safest city in the United States. Those who are of a more commercial bent may well be interested to know that Bill Bratten accomplished this without an increase in his budget.

Within these two years, murder rates fell 50%, theft fell 35% and public approval rates rose from 37% to 73%. Crucially, these changes lasted beyond Bill Bratten himself, suggesting that he had changed the culture and not relied on personal brilliance. Also, his record was not a one off. He was not like the football manager who becomes flavour of the month following a good cup run or exceeded expectations within the league. Only then to be poached by a rival team who discovered the magic had not followed long with his humungous contract. Bill Bratten's success was not simply a special time and place. His methods have resulted in significant changes over a thirty year career in various parts of policing across New York and Los Angeles. Indeed the British government is now courting him, keen to witness a repeat of his achievements on this side of the Atlantic.

This all suggests that the effects are resultant on his methods rather than charisma, and as such can be applied elsewhere. Wherever Bill Bratten has plied his trade, he has used a technique known as Tipping Point Leadership. What we shall do is to explore this in a little more detail, look at the challenges that Bill Bratten faced and how he achieved his remarkable success.

At this point I am reminded of the countless advertisements that saturate our television coverage each January, and other self help guides that promise us all wealth, happiness, health, success (delete as appropriate) in just 'these three simple and easy follow steps'. This kind of fair has never excited me greatly. So it is with a little gulp I shall now introduce the four steps to the Tipping Point, and describe how super-cop Bill used these to such effect. The four steps are:

1. Break through the cognitive hurdle
2. Sidestep the resource hurdle
3. Jump the motivational hurdle
4. Knock over the political hurdle

In order to develop Tipping Point Leadership, and the following change in culture, we need to explore these four steps in greater detail. The first being to break through the cognitive hurdle. When trying to communicate the need for change, leaders tend to offer facts and figures to justify their cause. These are impersonal and less effective at getting people to understand the need for change. People with well performing units feel unjustly criticised, whilst those with underperforming units are more likely to feel insecure about their job and look to leave rather than invest their efforts and energy into solving problems. To counter this issue, Bratten got his managers to see the problem face to face.

As head of Transit Police, Bratten found out that none of his senior managers travelled to work by the subway. The managers didn't consider the subway to be a concern as the statistics showed only 3% of crimes were committed there and as they didn't use the subway they were insensitive to the issue. They were unaware of what people actually had to contend with. Gangs of youths marauding around stations, countless drunks and vagrants, aggressive beggars and overcrowding. It is not just crime, but the perception of crime that impacts upon people. To challenge this, Bratten began requesting that everyone, including himself, travelled to work using the subway. This forced the managers to realise the extent of the problem. Whilst there were few major crimes on the subway, the policing of this area had to change as it was unacceptable in its current status quo. It worked. Bratten's line managers finally understood the necessity of change and supported his measures with much greater vigour than they otherwise would have.

Back in our world of Safety, how can we use or apply this principle? Each job or site is different; each organisation has different challenges and changes that need to be implemented. It is impossible to try to list them all here, but the importance of getting those who are responsible for helping to implement change to see why changes are needed is clear.

Inductions are a frequently cited area in which there is scope for improvement. Many of those I have received have been painful, long, boring, taken from a script that is largely irrelevant and crucially prone to missing Safety critical information. Recently, I was asked whether I had my risk assessments and method statements with me when entering an office block to do a training course. This was because a prompt on the 45 minute long induction asked for them. The very pleasant man conducting this personal induction looked almost as if he hoped I had them. I did not. The irony of the fact that I was there to teach the very same man about risk assessment was not lost on me. If more managers had to receive or deliver inductions with the materials provided then the importance of developing these would be more obvious. The induction is the first opportunity to communicate Safety to the workforce. When considering the development of a more progressive and positive Safety culture, what do you think it communicates to visitors or sub contractors if the first messages they receive are generic, boring and irrelevant? Or, in a more positive vein, what do you think the impact would be if a relevant, engaging induction process was implemented instead?

Through the winter many construction sites become wet and muddy, meaning drying rooms and welfare facilities become very important to the workforce. A strong leader may wish to invite the appropriate managers to a site visit for the day. These managers may suddenly appreciate how important communal drying rooms and welfare facilities are, when the more spacious offices with tea making facilities are only available offsite. How effective would that be at breaking through the cognitive hurdle?

Now the necessary people are suitably engaged and motivated, the next step is to 'sidestep the resource issue'. Once an organisation has agreed on the need or desire to change, they then face the reality of finite resources. This is true when the times are good, and in the age of austerity this is even more so. Often this results in a modification of objectives, dilution of strong changes and as a result demotivates the staff that you have just worked hard to motivate. However, Bill Bratten did not do this. His amazing results were achieved with no increase in resources, and sometimes with even fewer resources. He achieved this by ingenious use of existing resources and by altering the way in which they were implemented.

Back at the Transit Police in New York, it had become standard operating procedure to have a police presence at each entrance point to each station. Bratten changed this to focus his resources on the crime 'hot spots'. In order to prevent the relocation of crime he also moved more officers out of uniform into plain clothes. This meant that criminals learnt that the lack of uniformed officers did not mean there was no police presence whilst allowing him to devote more man power to the places where crime was much more likely to occur.

Bratten's ingenuity was not restricted to deployment of his staff. He realised that the amount of paperwork his officers had to do was more than restrictive. It was a motivation not to arrest, as each arrest required sixteen hours to process. Bratten cut that to just one, allowing his officers more time to do what they should be doing; police.

I am confident that this last paragraph would immediately translate into the world of Safety. I lose track of how many site managers, project managers and Safety officers complain that they are tied down to their desk with prohibitive amounts of paperwork. Systems have migrated over time and often created duplication or unnecessary paperwork (like my friend with the form filling to hand over the keys that we met earlier). This could be reviewed, slimmed and not one ounce of Safety or compliance removed from them, allowing people to focus on actual Safety matters than forms.

This is an opportune moment to acknowledge the irony of using a Policing example to extrapolate Safety based ideas. Health and Safety has historically been seen as policing both by the workforce and overzealous Safety professionals like Sergeant Safety and The Official. When I mention Bratten creating ways to enable his workforce to police, this should not be directly transposed into Safety. A Safety professional or site manager has to enforce and ensure standards without doubt, but also enable, coach and advise to improve Safety.

The third step involved in Tipping Point leadership is 'jumping the motivational hurdle'. This essentially means that once we have identified the changes, established support from the people who shall help implement these changes and ensured that our resources are as effectively deployed as possible – how can we get the remainder of the workforce to buy into the changes? Classically it has been referred to as 'workforce engagement' in Health and Safety.

Bratten considered it impossible and futile to try to get every single member of the police department to buy into his changes. Instead he identified key influencers who would convey his changes and messages. He also ensured that each change was couched in an attainable way.

Central to his methodology of culture change, Bratten used the 'scale free networks' that were in abundance within his organisation. Do similar networks reside within our worlds? I would suggest that when considering Safety performance an overwhelming majority of people conform, but there is nearly always a disproportionate amount of power within key individuals that skew the perception and performance of Safety. It is useful to remember that influencers do not necessarily have to be influential within a hierarchy and could operate at any position or function within a company, from director to labourer. I have seen behavioural initiatives launched with great fanfare, the beloved road show and a plethora of rebranded mugs and stationary only to be negated completely by the network effects of influential people from around the organisation. Rather than 'sheep dip' every single person within an organisation, identifying and engaging with the main influential people with the appropriate level of connections will be much more likely to help convey the changes planned.

The fact that the changes were considered attainable is important. There is a saying 'the elephant must be eaten bite by bite'. This means that should someone be asked if they could eat an elephant it would be considered woefully too big and impossible, but broken down each bite is possible (hence the term 'bite-sized'). Bratten had a phrase that he'd make the street of New York City safe "block by block, precinct by precinct, borough by borough." This is the polar opposite of what I witness regarding behavioural Safety initiatives, where the road show boasts some sort of mantra along the lines of 'zero accidents', 'perfect Safety', etc. Whilst this is a noble aim, it is too vast and abstract. It is considered impossible and so not believed by the workforce. If our aims are as big as this, our goals should be small. They should be realistic and targeted to the people as much as possible. Only when we accrue all of our small goals "block by block" may we realise we have actually achieved something much larger.

The final step in Bratten's Tipping Point leadership is to 'knock over the political hurdle'. Even if an organisation has reached its tipping point, there will still be people that resist change for their own personal or political reasons. Bratten overcame this in two ways. Firstly, he always appointed a senior insider, who would help identify people that were likely to support his changes and those who would silently sabotage them. This led to a swift change of guard.

This is particularly pertinent within Health and Safety. Given the historical development of Health and Safety and the legacy identified within the first section of this book, one might suspect that the upper echelons of a Safety department are most likely to be populated with people who are of a less progressive bent. This is not entirely true. There were one or two humans on Jurassic Park, but there was also the odd dinosaur. Whilst it is true that 'young cardinals vote for an old pope', a young or progressive pope should want to ensure his cardinals are with him on his journey and the changes he wants to make.

Bratten realised that he could not cull all of the dinosaurs in the New York police department, as there would not be enough people left to do the policing. So those who remained were faced with undisputable facts to challenge their long standing dogma and orthodoxy. Between this and the positive network effects Bratten was enabled to implement the changes he wished and reap the results that duly followed wherever he worked.

With some bold measures, thinking not clouded by doctrine, the use of networks and efficient use of resources Bill Bratten has changed the culture across a vast organisation. He faced similar obstacles that Health and Safety professional's encounter when aiming to improve the culture of Safety within their workplace. Bill Bratten proved it. It can be done.

The tragic case of Elaine Bromiley

At this point in our discussion about culture and how we can try to change things for the better, I would like to share with you the tragic true story of Elaine Bromiley.

On 29th March 2005, Elaine Bromiley, a 37 year old mother of two, reported to hospital for routine surgery on her nose. A senior nurse checked in Mrs Bromiley first thing in the morning. Mrs Bromiley mentioned that she had a fused bone in her neck and was immediately assured that that would not be an issue.

8.30

Mrs Bromiley entered the anaesthetic room to undergo the set up of routine monitoring for her during the procedure, as is standard for someone undergoing general anaesthetic. Mrs Bromiley was attached to an ECG machine to monitor her heart rate, a blood pressure cuff to measure blood flow throughout the procedure, a pulse oximeter to monitor the level of oxygen in the blood and a cannula in her left hand through which the anaesthetic was to be administered. She was ready for her general anaesthetic.

08.35

The anaesthetic was administered. The anaesthetist was unable to insert the tube to secure Mrs Bromiley's airway so gave her more anaesthetic to relax the jaw, but was still unable to fit different sized tubes.

08.37

At this stage, Mrs Bromiley's oxygen level began to deteriorate and she began to turn blue. Her oxygen saturation at this time was 75% (anything less than 90% is significantly low) and her heart rate was raised.

08.39

The oxygen saturation continued to deteriorate to a very low level (40%) over the next minute. Attempts to ventilate the lungs with 100% oxygen using a facemask and oral airway proved unsuccessful.

08.41-08.43

It was still proving near impossible to ventilate the lungs and the oxygen saturation remained perilously low at around 40%. The heart rate had declined to 69 beats per minute with a downward trend continuing to the low 40's. This is typical of what happens to a body when there is a lack of oxygen to the heart and brain. The Consultant anaesthetist who had an excellent reputation with his peers administered a drug to combat the slow heart rate and was joined by one of his colleague Consultant anaesthetists who had been informed of the difficulties.

08.45

An exploratory camera was used to explore the throat. The voice box was obscured which meant that the tracheal intubation would be very difficult or impossible. The oxygen saturation remained very low. By about this time, other staff had been summoned to the anaesthetic room to provide any necessary assistance. An experienced surgeon, specialising in Ear Nose and Throat surgery, also entered the anaesthetic room at about this time. Between attempts at placing a breathing tube, ventilation with oxygen via a facemask remained very difficult and Mrs Bromiley's oxygen levels remained perilously low. The situation now was categorised as 'can't intubate, can't ventilate' and is a recognised emergency in anaesthetic practice.

08.47-08.55

Further attempts at intubation were made using different equipment by both the anaesthetic Consultants, but were not successful as the larynx could not be seen. One then attempted to locate the larynx with a fibre-optic flexible scope, but this was unhelpful was unable due to blood obscuring the view. At this time, Mrs Bromiley's oxygen saturation level remained very low at 40% and the heart rate again was beginning to slow again.

08.55

The insertion of an intubating laryngeal mask allowed some ventilation, though it was still difficult to ventilate the lungs adequately.

09.00

The insertion of the intubating laryngeal mask improved matters and the oxygen saturation rose to 90%, some 25 minutes after it had initially fallen below this level.

09.03-09.09

Attempts were made to insert a tracheal tube through the intubating laryngeal mask, as the device is designed. The team failed to pass the intubating tube as they were unable to pass the scope through the end of the laryngeal mask (a recognised problem with this device). During these attempts, the oxygen level was unstable dipping down to 49% on occasion, but at no time did it exceed 90%.

09.10

In view of the problems encountered, it was decided to abandon the proposed surgery and allow Mrs Bromiley to wake up from her anaesthetic.

09.13-09.29

During this time, the anaesthetic was stopped and spontaneous breathing began (up till that time, the lungs had been ventilated by squeezing the bag on the anaesthetic machine). The laryngeal mask was removed and an oral airway inserted. Oxygen saturations gradually improved reaching near normal levels of 95%. Throughout this time, the blood pressure was markedly elevated and the heart rate was also very high (up to 152 bpm). Once the Consultant anaesthetist in charge was happy that Mrs Bromiley was breathing satisfactorily with the oral airway in place, she was transferred to the recovery room. At this time, the Consultant thought that Mrs Bromiley was showing signs of recovery and was breathing with a normal pattern. In total, during the attempts at intubation, Mrs Bromiley's oxygen saturation was extremely low (at or less than 40%) for around 20 minutes.

9.30

Mrs Bromiley was admitted to the recovery room at 09.30. The recovery staff had been aware of the problems that had occurred and were informed by the Consultant that he would expect Mrs Bromiley to recover consciousness slowly. After a short while with Mrs Bromiley, the Consultant left the recovery room to continue the operating list. The nurses were far from happy with Mrs Bromiley's condition. Even nearly one hour after admission to the recovery room, there was no sign of improvement in consciousness. Mrs Bromiley's breathing was erratic. The blood pressure was also unpredictable with swings from very high to low and the oxygen levels were unstable. Most concerning to the recovery staff were periodic episodes of movement that looked like fits. These were associated with further swings in measured parameters. These are signs of cerebral irritation and require prompt, appropriate action.

On several occasions, the recovery staff asked the Consultant to come to see Mrs Bromiley, but that was not always possible as he had already started to anaesthetise the next patient on the operating list. On occasion, a second Consultant came to see the patient, but he, quite legitimately, had a duty of care to his own patients. The exact times when requests were made of the Consultant are not recorded, but it is clear that the recovery staff felt that Consultant should have been more readily available to deal with any problems.

Concerns increased and eventually it was decided that Mrs Bromiley needed to be transferred to the Intensive Care Unit. As both Consultants were unavailable, (another Anaesthetist) attended to supervise the transfer. This took place at about 11.00 and Mrs Bromiley was transferred. At this time, she was in an unstable condition though was still breathing on her own. On admission to the intensive care unit at, it was clear that Mrs Bromiley had suffered marked brain damage and urgently required to be put onto a ventilator. Again there were problems with placing a tracheal tube, but finally it was possible to insert one through her nose and into her trachea.

Mrs Bromiley's condition did not improve and her clinical course resulted in her ultimate death. There was clear evidence of severe cerebral damage through her time on the Intensive Care Unit.

I apologise for the overtly medical language within the timeline of events, detailed medical knowledge is not required for our purposes. This is a tragic case of a lady who expected a routine, low risk procedure and ended up dying as a result of a complication, but why?

There was certainly not an issue with competency. The doctors involved were highly trained and well thought of by their peers. The cost of educating and training them would have run into the millions of pounds. There was no issue with the pre-operation checks and assessments. The identification of the major hazards by the Consultant prior to the operation were considered to be appropriate. There was no issue with the safe system of work prior to the operation. Whilst there are various ways to perform such procedures, the systems adopted by the Consultant were considered to be entirely appropriate.

The problems began when things did not go to plan, and the subsequent decision making. The Difficult Airway Society (DAS) had published guidelines to assist anaesthetists when it is difficult to intubate the patient. The primary concern is to ensure adequate oxygenation as soon as possible instead of continuing with the attempted intubation as the Consultant did with Mrs Bromiley. Mrs Bromiley suffered low levels of oxygen for over twenty minutes before the Consultant changed his plan and wake Mrs Bromiley up from her general anaesthetic. Standard teaching would suggest that this should be the case within three minutes. The Consultant stated in interviews afterwards that he had lost track of time and was unaware of how long had passed.

There was also an issue with people following the standard procedures despite them not being appropriate in this event. Mrs Bromiley should have been transferred directly to the Intensive Care Unit rather than being taken to the Recovery Room.

To revert back to our analysis of human failure, there were no obvious violations. There were no conscious thought processes that led to a deliberate deviation from a known rule or procedure. Indeed, all decisions made were trying to adhere to the systems and rules. A critic of this supposition may cite that the failure to follow the DAS guidelines and concentrate on the levels of oxygenation sooner would constitute a violation rather than an error, but this simply serves to underline the critique of this theory. I refer back to the 'computational capabilities' Herb Simon discussed. Simply saying 'follow the system' does not provide an adequate analysis of the real world. There was no one involved with this awful case that did not fully apply themselves or try their upmost to achieve a positive outcome.

There is another important issue raised by this case. The nurses were able to recognise the gravity of the situation, but were not empowered to elevate their concern. In Health and

Safety there is much work to be done regarding workforce engagement. Years of enforcement from Sergeant Safety and The Official have certainly not helped in many of these cases, but the power of individuals at all levels to have a positive impact is immense. This is referred to as 'flattening hierarchies'. Companies begin as flat organisations, with little distance between the managing director and the labourer (it is often the same person), but as companies grow a hierarchy becomes necessary for effective management. The empowerment of people at all levels of an organisation to flatten the hierarchy and use their voice, especially on Safety critical matters, could prevent significant loss.

It would be interesting to see just how quickly the perception of Health and Safety would change with the adaptation of a proactive Safety culture and an empowered and engaged workforce. Would we soon double take with incredulity when The Official tried to rear his prehistoric head in the same way that I do when my friend lights up his electronic cigarette in the pub, because it's just not done like that anymore?

The story of Sir Chris Hoy and a frog

This section begins to analyse the current accepted conventions within behavioural Safety, look at the limitations of these conventions and how people have changed organisational cultures successfully. In so doing, we have begun to shine a torch on ways in which it may be more effective to change a organisations Safety culture and not rely on rational human behaviour within the decision making process. I would like to draw one final element of food for thought as well as pave the way towards our final section.

The aim of behavioural Safety is to improve an organisations Health and Safety performance, in part by improving their Safety culture. This goal is a strategic, big picture approach where we try to align our moral beliefs into organisational norms. This is Safety from a macro level.

Our final section shall look more at the process of an individual's decision making, i.e. Safety at the micro level. These two perspectives do not stand separately like a pair of Dubai skyscrapers, but are connected. To explain this further we shall examine the two protagonists in the chapter title. Sir

Chris Hoy and a frog can help us understand behavioural change and successful cultural change within organisations.

Firstly, let us begin with the story of the frog. The frog looks at Safety on the micro level. Anyone that has attended one of my behavioural workshops shall no doubt be familiar with the frog, but allow me to explain once again here. A frog is a cold blooded creature. As a result its body temperature changes to match that of its environment. Now at this point, I probably ought to make it quite clear to anyone that has not attended one of my behavioural workshops that I do not demonstrate the following process live within my training. A call to the RSPCA is not necessary, I promise.

If you place a frog into a bowl of water that is at room temperature it will happily sit there as if it were sitting in a clear pond. If you have a bowl of boiling water into which you attempt to place the frog, it will immediately recognise the danger and hop away, which is an obvious and sensible reaction to such a threat. However, should the bowl with the cool water in it that our first frog is sitting in begin to slowly heat up, then the frog shall adjust its body temperature automatically to that of the water. This will continue until the frog literally boils to an unfortunate end.

The metaphor from this graphic tale from our Health and Safety perspective is relatively straight forward. The greatest danger often comes not from our ability to recognise inherently dangerous environments from the outset, but from environments that change slowly over time. I have often heard the phrase:

"Safety goes out of the window towards the end of the job."

It is the long term, small, changes that individually may not seem to matter greatly that begin to add up, incrementally increasing the levels of risk people may be exposing themselves to. Most dangerously of all, the same people may well be oblivious to the effect that these changes have had and the risks they are taking. This process is called 'scope creep', and can have a considerable impact of Health and Safety within an organisation or project.

Now I shall neatly traverse from the amphibian to the Olympian; the iconic powerhouse of cycling that is Sir Chris Hoy. Although in truth we shall more broadly at British Cycling. Cycling has never been so popular within this country. Names such as Chris Froome, Mark Cavendish and Sir Bradley Wiggins are all now extremely well known, but

British Cycling has not always received such notoriety. The change is simple and is down to success. A Britain had never won the Tour de France before Sir Bradley Wiggins did in 2012, followed just twelve months later by Chris Froome winning the yellow jersey. At the London Olympic games our Cycling teams were not simply the best, but almost demoralisingly so for their competitors. How had the Brits become so much better than the rest? What had they done? What had changed? There was even the near shrill accusation from their French counterparts that the team had managed to get their wheels more round. A gripe I particularly enjoyed I must confess.

Whilst it sounded a rather churlish claim from the French team, they had at least identified something. Whilst Sir Chris powered to his sixth and final Olympic gold medal as a result of his physical excellence and dedication, it would not be entirely surprising if the man behind the golden throne, Sir Dave Brailsford, had secretly reinvented the wheel. He hadn't of course. What he had done, with a forensic brilliance, was quietly reinvent everything else.

I imagine Brailsford would have been the ideal type of man to oversee the war effort at Bletchley Park. Tasking a wealth of our best and brightest to find answers to questions they had not yet thought of. In the absence of such a requirement for his remarkable vision and skill set he found himself instead as the head of British Cycling.

Brailsford's right hand man, central to Team GB's medal haul was Matt Parker. Parker was the 'Head of Marginal Gains', British Cycling were already world class, but they wanted to get better and be the very best. Marginal gains work best when already operating at a high level. They do not take the person that is 10th to become champion like a good chemist with an array of performance enhancing substances may. Marginal gains can make the difference between being on the third step of the podium and the top one. Rather than set a large, ambitious, daunting goal which may or may not be achievable, such as improving performance by 600% within two Olympic cycles (2 to 12 gold medals), they aimed to identify solutions to produce just 1% increase in performance. Some of the marginal gains that Parker is credited for introducing are heated pants which stopped rider's legs from cooling between warm up and race, and increasing the amount of cherries in the athlete's diets for the beneficial anti-oxidants that they contain. The impact was the inverse of that of the frog. Sir Chris Hoy and the rest of team GB benefitted from the accumulation of all the marginal gains. As individual changes these may not have seemed worthwhile, but cumulatively those gains added up to something very noticeable indeed.

So in our bid to achieve our Safety July, it is probably not the best idea to set large goals such as 'zero accidents'. Instead we should be using proven models of transforming organisational cultures 'block by block' and welcome the cumulative power of marginal gains to help us go from good to great.

In our final section, we shall try to identify some behavioural marginal gains; by using the latest in behavioural research how can we find our own improvement in performance by the odd few per cent. We shall do so with "nudges."

Section Three:

Soft power; Safety nudges

What is 'nudge'?

In the previous section we considered the concept of economic rationality and how the theory that all accidents are preventable is flawed with our current understanding of human decision making. We also looked at the power of marginal gains and how accumulation of small changes can help our Safety performance creep towards its overall objective.

As part of this consideration we deviated firmly off the track of Health and Safety academia and branched into other fields, primarily economics. The study of behavioural economics has the analysis of decision making central to it. This is closely related to behavioural psychology, both areas which could be mined as a rich ground of knowledge and research when considering behavioural Safety. As part of this quest, we came across works by John Maynard Keynes and Herb Simon; the godfather of behavioural economics. In particular we studied his re-assessment of what constitutes 'rational' in the real world. This then followed into the idea of networks, part of which was used to remarkable success by super-cop

Bill Bratten to help him change culture and performance across police departments in the United States of America.

Having looked at Health and Safety from the macro perspective this last section shall zoom in and consider behaviour and Safety at the micro level. At the level of individual people and individual decisions. Herb Simon has spawned many disciples who have taken his ideas of behaviour and decision making and built a stream of evidence. It is to these scientists who straddle the divide between economics and psychology that we now turn.

This section does not solely focus on the concept of nudges, but the work of the authors of "Nudge" and their peers shall be used to develop our understanding of behaviour to a greater extent. If you have had any experience of behavioural Safety training, you are probably familiar with some key themes. The themes of autopilot, habit and attention blindness are all certainly valid (the video with the Gorilla, which some people still like to brandish excitedly in the hope that failing to spot the Gorilla is new and revelatory). However I feel like there has been very little to develop the narrative and understanding further, despite a proliferation on the topic in other fields. It is my intention to join some of those isolated dots a little, and deepen peoples understanding of how behaviour can affect Safety.

'Nudge: improving decisions about health, wealth and happiness', was published in 2008. The authors were Richard Thaler and Cass Sunstein. Thaler was based from the University of Chicago and held the seat of Professor of Behavioural Science and Economics. Sunstein was Professor of Jurisprudence at University of Chicago Law School, Department of Political Science. The book was a huge success.

Nudges are essentially incentives. In economics, the price of something is the most often used incentive to do or to not do something. They use psychology to more effectively incentivise people's decision making. If Bill Bratten and his Tipping Point Leadership is the structural mechanism to help implement a behavioural Safety initiative, then the Safety nudge is the soft power to help supplement it. We probably all know where we would like Safety to be, we may now begin to have an idea of some who's and how's; the nudges are to ease the process and make it is impactful as possible.

The idea of nudges may not sit too comfortably with some. The sense of liberties being invaded by a faceless establishment can understandably create a sense of unease. I do not see nudges to act in that way or perform that function. Given the frailty of the human condition that we have already discussed, as well as the propensity for human error, nudges help use to guide our decision making when it is most likely be vulnerable. It is therefore helpful to be aware of when nudges are required and when they will be most effective.

The next part of our analysis owes more to 'Deal or No Deal' than HSE Guidance notes, but is helpful when we consider decision making under risk. Whilst Noel's knitwear fuelled road shows of the 1980's may not have provided Safety managers the greatest of role models when launching behavioural based initiatives, at least he is now providing us with some value.

If humans were perfect, rational beings our decision making would be faultless and entirely predictable as per the classical economic definitions. Thaler and Sunstein use two descriptors to highlight the difference; 'econ' and 'human'. The econ is a perfectly rational creature, with which the classic distinction of human failure is used. Humans behave and decide things in a less (economically) rational way.

We have already considered the rationality of human decision making, but let me provide you with another example. I shall provide you with a simple choice to make, between two options. First I will offer you £80. No strings or conditions attached, just a straight £80 in your pocket (at this point I should remind you that this is an entirely hypothetical offer). Alternatively I will offer you a gamble where you have an 80% chance of winning £100 and a 20% chance of winning £10. Which option do you prefer? A vast majority of people would take the sure thing; the guaranteed £80. However, analysis of the two options shows that the expected value of the second offer is £82. As such, this is the more preferable option to take. And yet our brains will insist that the former is still a better decision. This is precisely the gamble Noel and the banker play out each and every day.

We need another way to analyse human rationality rather than that of the econ mindset. Luckily, we have one.

What makes humans likely to take risks?

Warning: this chapter involves a number of theories, economists and scenarios. However, if we manage to come through the other side we may begin to understand a little more about the psychology of risk taking. The first economist/mathematician we shall briefly meet is Mr Bernoulli. Bernoulli is a well regarded and prolific mathematician who was seminal in the development of Utility Theory. Utility Theory is the first port of call when we examine the psychology of decision making and has its roots dating back over two hundred years. Utility Theory uses gambles as examples of choices to be made, which contain an uncertain outcome. It uses the rational economic agent, the 'econ' as its basis and remains the central most important theory in social sciences to this day.

Two psychologists, Daniel Kahneman and Amos Tversky decided to study why 'humans' make more risky decisions than 'econs'. They began by using the role playing gambles that Utility Theory would, but tried to find the intuitive human response rather than the economically rational one. Following five years of research they published 'Prospect Theory: An analysis of decision under risk'. Prospect Theory essentially modified Utility Theory to take into account the human factor in decision making.

Imagine how you would feel if you gained £1,000. Now imagine how you'd feel if you lost £1,000. Utility Theory states that a person would experience equal amounts of pleasure (utility) from the first option as they would loss (disutility) from the second. Utility Theory did not allow for any differences between losses and gains. This does not correspond to the real world. Consider the following choices;

Option 1: Which do you choose, A or B?

A: Receive £900.

B: A 90% chance of getting £1,000.

Option 2: Which do you choose, A or B?

A: Lose £900

B: A 90% chance of losing £1,000.

In the first option, most people are risk averse. The certainty of gaining £900 outweighs the 90% possibility of gaining £1,000. However, in the second option most people go for option B. The certainty of losing £900 is a strong motivator and so people are more willing to take the chance of the gamble in option B. The difference in attitudes towards risk with favourable and non favourable outcomes shows the discrepancy between 'econ' and 'human' decision making.

Here are two more decisions for you to consider.

Option 1: You are given £2,000. Which do you choose?

A: 50% chance to win £2,000.

B: A guaranteed £1,000.

Option 2: You are given £4,000. Which do you choose?

A: 50% chance to lose £2,000.

B: A guaranteed loss of £1,000.

Under Utility Theory, both of these problems are identical. The choices are either to accept a guaranteed £3,000, or gamble when there is an equal chance that you could be either £2,000 or £4,000 better off. Interestingly, most humans would opt for option B in the first choice and option A in the second. People tend to be risk averse with gains, but risk takers with potential losses. The dynamic between probability, and gains and losses can be shown in the figure below, generated by Kahneman and Tversky called the 'Fourfold Pattern'.

	Gains	**Losses**
High Probability	95% chance to win £10,000 Fear of disappointment **Risk averse**	95% chance to lose £10,000 Hope to avoid loss **Risk seeking**
Low Probability	5% chance to win £10,000 Hope of large gain **Risk seeking**	5% chance to lose £10,000 Fear of large loss **Risk averse**

The top two rows provide an example of a gamble, like the ones we have already encountered. The third row suggests the main emotion that this gamble generates. The forth row states whether the decision is likely to be risk averse or risk seeking.

From our Health and Safety perspective, the two cells of greatest importance are the bottom left and the top right. The cell in the bottom left is 'The Lottery Cell'. People are willing to take a risk in the hope of a large gain, acknowledging that the likelihood the outcome occurring is low. The top right cell is 'The Dice Cell'. This is where people are willing to roll the dice, accepting that there is a good chance of making things worse in the hope of avoiding a large loss.

When looking at accidents and incidents, we see human behaviour can mimic the behaviour in both of these cells. Although within Safety we work in the inverse of this model which can confuse labels of gains or losses. Sometimes people take the chance, maybe cutting a corner to get the 'win' of finishing the task more quickly, or accept the risk because "it'll never happen to them". This is the cell in the bottom left, 'The Lottery Cell'. Alternatively, people may find themselves in an unexpected situation and faced with the enormity and complexity of a situation be tempted to gamble in the hope that the situation can be retrieved, even if this is unlikely.

If we were to apply these two decisions into the classical analysis of human failure they would be considered violations and therefore reinforce the idea that all accidents are preventable. However, the choices within this chapter have shown that the human decision making is not always able to analyse the optimal or rational choice. People can end up in either of the cells which support risk taking behaviour without necessarily knowing it. The optimal choice is not the important aspect of the decision making process, but the reference point from which the win or loss is judged from.

Our challenge is to identify how and when humans may be likely to roll the dice or buy a lottery ticket and develop mechanisms around them to make this set of circumstances less likely. This will encourage a more risk averse mindset. The culture of an organisation is important to this end and the requisite use of networks, but what can we do at a personal level?

The importance of a belief

Before I start, I would like to reassure you that the countless late nights I have spent in Premier Inns up and down the land writing this book have not induced a marked impairment of my mental faculty. Neither have I lost enthusiasm for the naming of the sections of this book and so decided to regurgitate and recycle previous efforts in the hope that nobody would realise. Rather, I see this section as a continuation of the conversation started in section one of this book, when we looked at the broad ideas that currently exist with behavioural Safety and the importance placed upon beliefs as a key component in generating the positive change in Safety performance we strive for.

We previously looked at how we can try to change the Safety culture within an organisation. We also considered the flaws with the existing orthodoxy, primarily that the mechanisms espoused work on the presumption of an economic model of rational human behaviour. This then begun our journey, exploring ideas within other scientific fields that consider actual human behaviour and how that can be used to help generate the change in culture we aspire to.

At this level, beliefs have relevance. A company wishing to cultivate this progressive approach to Health and Safety must have shared belief amongst the key decision makers to undertake those changes. However, we also looked how it is not necessary for everyone within the organisation to have a positive Safety belief. The use of networks can create a tipping point that allows change in culture to occur. So, at no point am I saying that beliefs are not important when trying to initiate behavioural Safety. They serve a valuable function at management level and the development of a program of culture change.

In the second section of this book, when we briefly looked at the importance of a belief, I explained how beliefs directly affect behaviour, the conclusion being that a person with positive Safety beliefs would adjust their behaviour; accidents would dramatically reduce and our utopian Safety July would be upon us. This is the prevailing wisdom within behavioural Safety. Numerous case studies and workshops can be found which will state that a key objective is to impress upon people the direct correlation between beliefs and behaviours.

This is the moment when I bring in the word "but." The problem with the process just mentioned is that scientific research would suggest that there is no direct causality between beliefs and behaviours. In order to support this notion, I shall begin to delve even deeper into the psychology of decision making. When someone is sitting in a meeting or training environment discussing behavioural Safety, it is fair to expect a degree of rationality within the decision making. Unfortunately the decisions people make in the moments before an accident are very different, and don't necessarily possess the same level of logic. In fact decisions immediately surrounding an accident operate within another part of the brain (see the section "The man with two brains" for more discussion on how the brain can react to stimulus).

Central to understanding this, is the concept which Nick Chater refers to as "The mind being flat." He is the Professor of Behavioural Science at Warwickshire Business School and advisor to the Governments Behavioural Insight Unit, otherwise referred to as the 'Nudge Unit'. We tend to think that our decisions are made as a result of our beliefs that are fixed, creating a very structured, reliable and rational world. It would appear instead that our beliefs are rather far from being fixed and can be highly variable indeed. This is quite an abstract idea, so allow me to first describe a couple of experiments that demonstrate how little beliefs affect decision making, and in fact how beliefs are created by our mind to justify our decisions.

Imagine sitting down with someone who presented two photographs portraits of a person to you and asked which person you preferred the look of. We would automatically assume that we will make our decision based on deeply held, static beliefs about appearance. An experiment explored this very premise, however after the chooser had made their decision, via a sleight of hand, they were then presented with the photograph of the person that they had rejected and asked to explain why they had chosen this photograph. At this point, we probably bristle at this slightly absurd scenario and automatically presume we shall notice the deceit. We would certainly not be able to provide reasons why we had just "chosen" that photograph because we didn't choose it and in fact rejected it in preference for another. The surprising thing is that a vast majority of people, about 85%, did not do this. They did not act in a rational manner. In fact, they were able to produce a number of reasons as to why they made their decision. Our minds began to rationalise our thought process and create a story to fit the scenario.

Now imagine I gave you another choice and another question. Which holiday would you choose between an expensive and exciting holiday and a cheap, fairly boring holiday? Perhaps a choice between Bali and Bournemouth? If you were like most people, you would choose the Bali option. However, in the experiments that asked this question, they then asked another large group of people a slightly different question; this time they were asked which of the two options would you reject? Now, if we possessed deep beliefs and preferences we would expect the answer this time to be Bournemouth as we just chose Bali as our preferred option, but this was now what the investigators found! People chose Bali again. When asked the same question in a slightly different way people made the opposite decision.

Often when we make decisions, there is no great process of introspection to search our beliefs and act accordingly. Rather we simply don't have a preference and actually create our reasoning afterwards. Beliefs don't affect people's decisions often, even if we can subsequently create a justification for the decision once it is made. With a bit more understanding of the psychology of decision making, and by relinquishing our hope in rationality and beliefs, we can begin to be more effective in having a positive impact on Health and Safety.

Ones and zeros baby

During the section "What makes humans likely to take risks?" I introduced Kahneman and Tversky's 'The Fourfold Pattern'. This offers insight into decision making and motivations of humans rather than econs. For a majority of the time, humans will be risk averse and in the healthier parts of the 'Fourfold Pattern', but sometimes will be willing to roll the dice or buy a lottery ticket. We now need to understand the psychology of the healthier aspects and what we can do to encourage humans to adopt this approach using nudges.

The first idea behind nudging is an obvious one. People like to win. Obviously the competitive edge in individuals can vary. My wife has still not fully recovered from a comeback of epic proportions during a rather competitive game of Scrabble whilst sitting on a balcony in Spain in 1989. Never in the history of mankind has the word 'quiz' been the source of such contention and anger, despite the fact that the word was wonderfully positioned on the triple word score, helping me to overcome the significant she had accrued over the course of the game and several San Miguel's.

There is a man who drinks in my local pub, not the one with the electronic cigarette, although he is there too. This one is a keen pub sportsman and is proficient at the main two pub sports of darts and pool. Having just scraped to another glorious victory over a leg of darts, despite only hitting double one at his ninth attempt, he would turn and dismiss any notion of indifferent throwing with the retort of "ones and zeros baby." It was either a win or a loss. And no extra points were given for anything else. Yup, people like a win alright.

Did you know that losing something makes people twice as miserable as they would be for gaining the exact same thing? This shows that people are loss averse. There have been many experiments that prove precisely this. In the experiments, the individuals of half a class are given a mug, usually with some insignia or motif to make it desirable. The other half of the class are then asked to examine one of those mugs. Then the class are asked to write down at what value they would sell the mug if they had one, or buy the mug if they didn't. The results consistently show that the people that have been given the mugs place a value on the mugs that is twice as much as the people who were not given the mugs would be willing to pay for them.

This shows that once I have a mug I don't want to let it go, but if I don't have one then I am not too concerned about joining in. This creates inertia. I am not likely to make a change and instead prefer to stay where I am doing what I am doing, even if I can see that the other option is preferable. Loss aversion can act as a king of nudge, encouraging us not make change even if a change is in our best interests. This is the top left cell in the 'Fourfold Pattern', where humans decide against the fear of disappointment and so refuse to change. It is also called the 'Head in the sand cell'.

When considering behavioural Safety initiatives this is a crucial factor. I have trained thousands of people in behavioural Safety and an overwhelming majority agree with the principles and morality of it. They hope for a 'Safety July'. Unfortunately this is countered with reluctance and a cynicism about what will actually happen. I remind you of a typical conversation I have that I introduced when discussing Safety People:

"That's all great mate. If it happens then I am in. Has this message been given to the Safety team?"

This was a standard opening to a conversation. I would insist that yes indeed the Safety team had been part of the program and received the same message.

"Well they don't believe it. They are still *****s" was a not untypical reply.

This increases the likelihood of people being risk averse, and staying with the behaviour they already have. To overcome this inertia we have to look what influencing factors we have around them. What are the network effects? Also, because people want to win, we need to make sure people experience the sensation of the win quickly to reinforce and perpetuate change. Can we show them a change and a benefit quickly rather than "zero accidents in five years" or other large corporate slogans? What can be witnessed by people 'block by block'?

The man with two brains

It is fair to say that my wife and I have rather different preferences with our desired television schedules. I have yet to fathom why she would choose not to spend her Monday evening watching Swindon take on Brentford, or fail to get excited about watching a near whole day of test cricket. My wife would prefer the latest revelations in Weatherfield or watch a customs officer trawl through suspect baggage at an airport. To my mind this is simply watching other people work. Each to their own, as they say. My wife is also terrible at watching a film and has a near perfect record of getting up after half an hour having proclaimed that the film was 'boring'. The only time I have ever known her to watch a film is during a flight where she is essentially strapped to a chair on a steel tube with little my way of alternatives.

Our last flight was such an example and we began to watch a rather mediocre film. To supplement our viewing pleasure I purchased a large bag of chocolate buttons. As I started feeling nauseated I realised that I had eaten enough chocolate. Without thinking I removed the bag from my fold down tray and put it away. My wife, rather than being cross about my lack of a consensual approach, turned and thanked me for removing them. Before I removed the chocolate, we had three choices. Eat all of the chocolate. Eat none of the chocolate. Eat some of the chocolate, which would probably have been followed by a bit more and a bit more. Eating all of the chocolate would have left us feeling ill for the remaining seven hours of the journey, which was our least preferable option. Yet this was the option that we were choosing. This is another example of how the human differs from the econ in terms of rational decision making.

To understand our apparently poor decision making, we need to understand a little more about the psychology of decision making and how our brains function. There are several psychologists that have labels to help describe similar processes. Dr Steve Peters, who is the noted sports psychologist that helped steer Ronnie O Sullivan to World Championship success as well working with both Liverpool FC and part of the England set up for the World Cup in Brazil, uses the phrases 'chimps' and 'humans'. Kahneman uses 'system 1' and 'system 2'. Thaler and Sunstein use 'planners' and 'doers', but also use a metaphor that I shall now adopt and explain.

When given a stimulus or choice, there are two parts of our brain, which can function and respond. The first is our considered way of responding, the way that we would probably hope to respond. This is 'system 2', 'human' or 'planner' depending on your particular taste in vodka, but I shall call it 'Spock'. Spock is concerned with our long term welfare, tries to make more strategic decisions, but has to combat the much stronger and immediate part of our brain. This is our 'system 1', 'chimp' or 'doer', but I shall refer to it as 'Homer', after Homer Simpson. Incidentally, Homer also happens to be what my family have nicknamed me for years for the same reason. Homer is automatic and responds emotively to stimulus. He is also much stronger than Spock, so easily shouts over his more considered thoughts. Homer is not a long term thinker and is only concerned with the immediate consequences of decisions. Temptation is a huge factor for him. Within all of us we have both Spock and Homer that are used in our decision making processes. On the aeroplane it was our Homer that happily continued to scoff the chocolate. It wasn't until the more strategic Spock shouted loud enough did we change our behaviour.

By the way, Homer is also very happy when not needing to think too hard, and so mindless tasks requiring little conscious thought, and a mindset of autopilot, suit Homer down to the ground. As anyone that has a vague understanding of The Simpsons knows, Homer and errors go hand in hand.

Where undesirable behaviour is the outcome of allowing Homer to make the decision, our challenge is to create a mechanism which shifts the thought process from the mindless, automatic response of Homer to one that requires more thought and time. We want to allow Spock to show his forte.

Two friends noticed that they were putting on weight. An increasingly sedentary lifestyle and travelling away with nights in hotels had helped contribute to this. To address this, the two friends made a deal to lose one stone in a year. If they failed, they had to give the other person £5,000. One year later, both men had lost the required stone. The game continued, whereby at any point they could call for a weigh in and should either one be over the target weight they had to pay a predetermined penalty immediately.

This acted as a nudge on their behaviour. Without this, the pair would have continued to eat poorly, exercise infrequently and put on more weight. However, the bet moved the decision away from Homer and allowed Spock to analyse the longer term welfare of the individual. The prospect of losing £5,000 was more powerful than the immediate gratification of an afternoon relaxing, rather going for a swim or run.

Leaving our decision making to Homer is potentially dangerous, given how reckless, short sighted and error prone Homer can be. It is Homer that makes accidents more likely to happen. We need to find ways in which we can negate Homer and allow Spock time to make decisions based on our long term welfare and nudge our behaviour just as the two friends losing weight.

One suggestion would be to revise how subcontractors are paid. Subcontractors typically do the majority of the actual work or production and also suffer accidents and loss. It is unlikely that large corporate goals, slogans and initiatives would have much resonance with sub contractors who work for many larger contractors. Punitive financial measures for poor Safety performance are too reactive, negative and likely to foster disengagement or outright hostility. Instead I would establish the terms of the contract with a percentage "extra" given for excellent Safety performance. This could be on an individual or group basis.

For example, I am Project Manager on a small construction site. I have some roof work, which needs to be completed. The sub contractors are 'GN Roofing' and the value of the contract is £10,000. On awarding the contract I offer GN Roofing a contract worth £7,000 with an additional £3,000 once the job is completed and in accordance to my Safety standards. The incentive should be sufficient to shift individual's mindset from their Homer to Spock, in order for them to earn their additional 30% payment and shift their behaviour to Safety July.

Sheep, smiles and frowns

This chapter is the little brother of the chapter about Network Theory. Scale Free Networks can be used to increase our chances of successfully changing culture using the disproportionate power of well connected, influential people. This chapter now zooms in to the personal level and the psychology of each link.

The simple fact is that people are easily nudged by other people. This is because we like to conform and fit in. The extent to which we will do this is quite astonishing. There have been many replications of experiments on social conformity, which consistently show that people will conform between 20-40% of the time in a simple task when the answer is blatantly wrong.

A typical conformity experiment is as follows. A group of six people congregate in a test of visual perception. The task is very simple. Each individual is given a card with a line on it. On a large screen three lines are projected upon it. The individual simply has to match their line with the line that is of identical length. The first three rounds follow as expected, each person makes their match aloud, in sequence, and everyone agrees with the choices made. However, on the fourth round, the first five people all make a glaringly obvious mistake. What would you do? When asked, most people answer that they would offer the correct answer. They are independent, intelligent people and would stick to their guns. This is the Spock response. The experiments showed repeatedly that people would defy their own senses and stick with the crowd between 20-40% of the time. They go with Homer. In private, individuals are less likely to conform, but in public we are not likely to risk disapproval from a peer group. Homer takes over. So how can we nudge our inner Homer to positive Safety behaviour?

There was a study into how powerfully people like to conform to what is the socially expected norm in San Marcos, California. It looked at household's energy consumption. Three hundred households were given information regarding their previous week's energy consumption and also given information about mean consumption of energy within the neighbourhood. The following week, households that had used less energy than average increased their consumption and households that used more than the average reduced their consumption. The lesson is clear; if we want to nudge people into displaying more positive behaviour do not let them know that their current performance is better than average.

Expect there was a more subtle nudge used as part of this study. As well as the written information about whether their household's consumption was above or below the average, half of the houses received an additional cue. This cue was an emoticon, either a smiley face or a frowning face. With this additional nudge, the households that had over consumed decreased their consumption the following week to an even greater degree than those without the emoticon. Similarly those households that had used less energy than the mean increased their usage, apart from those that received a smiley face. Their behaviour did not change and they maintained the preferable behavioural choice. Their energy usage remained below the mean level.

In a culture that has allowed Sergeant Safety and The Official to flourish and Safety communication to become increasingly negative, there is a huge amount of scope to improve. Safety communication and feedback needs to include, reinforce and recognise positive behaviours instead of just focussing on areas that are poor. This demonstrates a simple way in which we can positively reinforce behaviours with intelligent use of social nudges.

Given that the subject of feedback has reared it' head, I would like to share another psychological insight with you. This is referred to as 'regression to the mean'. Earlier, we met one of the leading behavioural psychologists; Daniel Kahneman. Kahneman retells a story about an occasion when he was training the Israeli Air Force about the psychology of effective training. In particular he taught how rewards for improved performance have greater impact than the punishment of mistakes. This approach shares the same principles to that of behavioural Safety initiatives and culture change programmes. I shall allow Kahneman to retell his story in his own words.

"When I finished my enthusiastic speech, one of the most experienced instructors in the group raised his hands and made a short speech of his own. He began by conceding that rewarding improved performance might be good for the birds, but he denied it was optimal for flight cadets. This is what he said: "On many occasions I have praised flight cadets for clean execution of some acrobatic manoeuvre. The next time they try the same manoeuvre they usually do worse. On the other hand, I have often screamed into a cadet's earphone for bad execution, and in general he does better on his next try. So please don't tell us that reward works and punishment does not, because the opposite is the case."

The flight instructor's attitude is not dissimilar to the kind of attitude and approach I encounter regularly within Safety related communication. The problem is that people with the same attitude as the flight instructor are fundamentally incorrect in their attempt to link cause and effect. The subsequent behaviour change had nothing to do with their feedback, but 'regression to the mean'. This phrase explains fluctuations in performance that are due to change in luck. Humans are not robots and so repetition is not an exact science. People that have a perfect performance will probably follow this with a poorer attempt; conversely people that under perform will probably improve their following attempt. This will occur irrespective of feedback offered. So when considering how effective your interventions are, it is prudent to take a longer term perspective and consider "what is their mean performance?" rather than focus on the fluctuations between each individual event.

I have an operative who usually displays positive behaviour and as a result receives positive feedback, but on one walk around the site I see that he is not wearing the correct PPE. Does this suggest that my positive feedback has not worked? If I give him a fairly stern rebuke and I see that the following time he has his PPE on correctly, does this demonstrate how effective my rebuke has been? Or is it the case that the operative would have regressed back to his mean performance anyway? The same questions can be applied to the inverse situation. An awareness of the mean performance will help us make better judgements about both behaviour and effective feedback.

Exercising Homer

Our psychological Homer is lazy. He likes immediate answers and short term gains. He also is much quicker and stronger than our internal Spock. If we are to design effective Safety strategies we need to understand that Homer is the one that is likely to make errors so we can design strategies around him. In order to do that we need to know how Homer reacts to things, so we are going to take Homer to the gym.

Our first game is simple. On the next page are a series of words. All you need to do is to shout out as quickly as possible whether they are written in lower case or upper case. However, if you are reading this on public transport I am not to be held accountable for the looks you may receive from fellow passengers if you begin to randomly shout out.

UPPER

LOWER

lower

up

LOW

neither

upper

LOWER

lower

YES

Not easy is it? This is because Homer likes the immediate answer and yet the information received is contradictory and too difficult for Homer. Let's try another, what is the first thought that comes to mind when you see this sign?

"Like"

Again, the conflicting messages confuse Homer and therefore encourage mistakes to be made. The things around us that nudge us into making choices are called 'choice architecture'. The previous exercises are examples of poor architecture. There is a classic example of good choice architecture, and it is found in a toilet in Amsterdam.

There is always an element of luck and risk involved when frequenting public toilets within any facility. Entrepreneur, Doug Kempel, designed an ingenious way to combat spillage that is found often in men's urinals. He placed a plastic fly in each bowl. The resulting target led to a reduction in spillage by 80%! Not only did this make the bathrooms more pleasant places to visit, there was a significant reduction of risk from slips, trips and falls and they required less cleaning with the use of hazardous chemicals. It is a different take on 'Safety starts at design', but an effective nudge none the less.

I saw another example when visiting my son in Edinburgh. Walking through the city centre and trying to circumnavigate the extensive road works for the impending tram system (I confess that I may at one point been caught more interested in the work in the middle of Princes Street than the impressive castle peering over us which is tragic I know), I noticed that there were signs on the road at pedestrian crossings saying "look left" or "look right." I had seen these signs before on my travels, but realised that I hadn't seen any of them anywhere near my sleepy, semi-rural peace with South Staffordshire. I wondered why. Each year, Edinburgh hosts millions of tourists from all over the worlds in sharp contrast to the southern parts of Staffordshire. Many of these tourists would have travelled from countries that do not drive on the left hand side of the road. As a result, their inner Homer would automatically look to the wrong direction in order detect cars, increasing the likelihood of a poor choice and walking straight into the path of an oncoming vehicle. The signage is a nudge to mitigate the chance of Homer sending a tourist under a Lothian bus. Given that Princes Street is not witness to serial road traffic accidents involving tourists in August it would seem to help.

There is another element to designing choice architecture if we are to try to nudge Homer into making better decisions. This is best understood by continuing to exercise Homer. The following game works better with two other people. Ask the first person the following questions (out of earshot of the second person ideally):

Is the height of the tallest Redwood tree more or less than 1,200 feet?

What is your best guess about the height of the tallest Redwood tree?

Now ask the second person the following questions:

Is the height of the tallest Redwood tree more or less than 180 feet?

What is your best guess about the height of the tallest Redwood tree?

These questions were used as part of an experiment. Unsurprisingly, the first group offered significantly higher answers than the second group, by 562 feet. This is because the number in the first question acted as an 'anchor' which Homer used because it was immediately available. The anchoring effect can have an impact of up to 55%, which is a considerable nudge.

Here is an example of anchors used in practice. A supermarket was running a promotion on cans of soup. On some days they displayed signs saying "Limit of 12 per person", and other day's signs saying "No limit per person."

What effect do you think the anchor or twelve cans had on shopper behaviour? With no limit in place, shoppers averaged three and a half cans. This doubled to seven cans when the limit was in place.

Depending on your work place, there may be a range of ways in which we can design choice architecture to promote more positive behaviour. Traffic management, signage and welfare facilities are potentially fertile breeding grounds for such ideas. There is another area of Health and Safety in which we can use our understanding of how Homer works to improve performance. Near miss reporting is something that has the potential to improve Safety performance although these systems are often met with some degree of resistance from the workforce. Most of these systems are deployed with a desire to get as many near misses reported as possible; there is no limit. The examples above would suggest that by using anchors we could nudge people to reporting more near misses. By placing an arbitrary limit and 'rationing' reporting individuals may be more likely to complete a report.

What time is it?

There is one final piece of psychology that it is useful to discuss in relation to our inner Homer and the propensity for us to be led into a situation where we make poor decisions. It goes back to the tragic case of Elaine Bromiley. You may remember that the Consultant Anaesthetist who was responsible overall for the operation continued trying to secure Mrs Bromiley's airway whilst her oxygenation levels continued to slide to a dangerously low level. The DAS guidelines stated that after three minutes of unsuccessfully securing a difficult airway the Anaesthetist should put their attention towards oxygen levels as the number one priority to stop the brain from becoming damaged. The Consultant, a highly regarded and supremely competent individual, continued to focus on securing the airway for over twenty minutes. This was central to the insult Mrs Bromiley tragically suffered and ultimately her death. How can we explain the Consultants actions and his confessed loss of time?

To understand this tragic error in time keeping we need to look at yet another theory. This time it is the Load Theory of Selective Attention and Cognitive Control, or more typically shortened to 'Load Theory'. Load Theory explains the effect on attention when executing tasks which require a high degree of focus or ability. The brain can respond to the task by giving its' full attention in order to execute it properly. However, if that is choice made, the brain is unable to maintain an awareness of what is going on around them, which is called 'situational awareness'. Alternatively, the brain can maintain a degree of situational awareness, but at a cost to the amount of cognitive effort applied to the task. We can have one or the other, but not both.

On training courses I play a game to allow delegates to experience this. Anyone would be able to replicate this easily enough. Using a pack of playing cards the delegates are asked to shout out "five" each time the card shown is exactly five more or five fewer in number than the previous card. For example, if I held up the two of clubs, and then the seven of hearts the correct response would be to shout "five" at that moment, but if I was then display a four of diamonds as my next card then the delegates would remain silent. After a short trial I begin the exercise, turning the cards over at a reasonable speed to warrant individual's total attention on the mental arithmetic. After completing the task (normally when I have gone through the whole deck) I ask the delegates how long they think that they were doing that. I am normally

165

greeted with confused looks as the delegates simply have no concept of how long they were playing. At best they can offer only a rudimental guess.

This is the same process that the Consultant Anaesthetist experienced. Focussing all of his mental ability on trying to secure Mrs Bromiley's airway he lost all sense of situational awareness. The passage of time, more than seventeen minutes longer than the guidelines state, with low oxygen levels resulted in Mrs Bromiley's death.

Load Theory is useful to understand and be aware of when considering situations in which people are likely to make poor decisions and/or mistakes. In high pressure situations, or when tasks require higher levels of attention, the operative is far more likely to experience a huge decrease in their situational awareness. This is where having developed an open culture with effective communication can help counter the potential danger. Also, the ability to flatten hierarchies mentioned earlier, to empower people to know to use their voice on Safety critical matters irrespective of their position within the hierarchy could be the vital nudge required to stop an event from occurring. After all; it's about trying to prevent all accidents.

Final thoughts

We have now reached the end of our journey. If this were a training course I would normally be watching for some classic tell tale signs that people are ready to leave, like jangling the car keys. That's normally a pretty clear cue, but before I draw this officially to a close, would like to offer a few final thoughts on the range of topics we have discussed. I did promise at the very beginning of this book that there would be no test at the end and shall be a man of my word.

We started this book with a bit of a reflective look at Health and Safety as a whole. I have been around Safety all of my professional life, as a worker and contractor and on the other side of the fence as a Safety professional and trainer. I have been lucky to enjoy nearly all of my work and have met some fantastic people along the way. My time has been filled with a lot of fierce craic. It is all of those hours of laughter and great characters that I think about when I approach Safety. It's about the people that get out of bed in a morning and work incredibly hard often doing dangerous, dirty and difficult jobs to provide for their family. People should not experience pain or loss as part of their working life. Having been around major accidents and sadly some fatalities, it is the worst place to be and one I would not wish upon anyone. I have met tens of thousands of people and discussed Health and Safety with them. An overwhelming majority agree and understand the importance of Safety and have no issue with Health and Safety in principle; they would love to be able to their jobs safely and not risk the kind of loss mentioned above.

It is disappointing that the phrase 'Health and Safety' has become a derogatory term, a punch line or slur. How can an endeavour with such solid morality have become a colloquial punch bag? Whatever our role is within industry, we should all examine ourselves and our beliefs about Safety. We should be asking ourselves if we can do more, whether our way of working is as effective as it can be in today's world and if we can remove the stigma associated with this crucial aspect of our work.

This book looked at behavioural approaches to Safety. There are many behavioural text books which provide a more rigorous explanation of why behaviour is important when improving Safety performance. There are central tenets, which anyone with an exposure to behavioural Safety approaches would probably be familiar, including ideas such as habits, autopilot and attention blindness. These factors are certainly valid and important.

Behavioural Safety also considers the distinction between conscious and unconscious thoughts; violations and errors. The accepted doctrine within behavioural Safety is that all accidents are preventable, as there is always some degree of violation within the causation analysis. To challenge and change conscious thoughts will lead us to the Health and Safety holy grail. As much as I share the hope for this Health and Safety holy grail, I honestly feel that this analysis is too simplistic.

The analysis relies on a concept of rationality which is the bedrock of classical economics. There is a considerable difference between what the economically rational agent would choose to do and what the human would choose to do. This is what academics refer to as 'bounded rationality'. If we are going to develop strategies that work in the real world we need to consider the human being and not the economically rationally agent. To this end, there has been an ever increasing field of research within behavioural economics and psychology, starting with luminaries Keynes and Simon and subsequently scientists like Kahneman, Thaler, Tversky, Sunstein and Ormerod to name just a few sources and inspirations behind this book.

To help us in our endeavour of our Health and Safety holy grail, we need to consider how to effectively change culture. This could be the culture of a large multi-national company, or a single site or project. It would appear that there are two aspects to this; information and influence. It is important to involve all people within the organisation to provide them with information and an understanding of where the aspired journey will take everyone. However, to simply undertake this process alone results in less change than hoped. This is due to the powerful negative network effects that would be present after years of disengagement with Health and Safety. To maximise our likelihood of succeeding in changing an organisational culture we must look at influence before information. The effective use of network effects is crucial to this end. We need to consider how we can reverse the negative network effects and harness this power to actively promote behavioural initiatives so that they can gain critical mass. Bill Bratten has been a very effective leader using networks to help him achieve such cultural change.

We can also use our ever greater understanding of the psychology of decision making to try to nudge use from making error prone choices. Inside our brains we have two systems that react to stimulus, one that is automatic, lazy, strong and quick. He is our internal Homer Simpson. Then there is our more analytical system, which likes to take into account our long term welfare. It is weaker and slower than Homer. Our internal Captain Spock therefore needs as much help as possible to reign in Homer before he gets us into mischief.

We can understand when we are more likely to react with economically irrational, risk taking decisions to help decide when we are more likely to require a nudge. Homer doesn't like to change so we need to get past that inertia, but remember Homer likes to conform, be part of the crowd and will respond strongly to a smile and a frown.

Finally, we looked at when our internal Homer, responding automatically, may struggle sometimes. Can we design choice architecture around this fact and subtle anchors to nudge us into more positive Safety behaviour? When the pressure is high and the level of difficultly considerable, we may lose some degree of awareness. This is where we need to have a culture when people know they can speak, irrespective of where they sit in rank and file. We must flatten the hierarchy and know that anyone within an organisation has the power to make a Safety critical intervention. If you ever think not to, or why should we bother, just remember the tragic case of Elaine Bromiley, a thirty two year old mother of two, and remember what Health and Safety is really all about.

Good luck.

Things to see or read

Baddeley S and James K. Owl, Fox, Donkey or Sheep: Political Skills for Managers. *Management Learning.* April 1987. 18: 3-19

Bernoulli D. Exposition of a New Theory on the Measurement of Risk. *Econometrica.* 1738. 22: 23-36

Buttolph M. Styles of Safety practice: Monks, mercenaries and missionaries (part 1). *Safety & Health Practitioner.* March 1999. 31-38

Chan Kim W and Mauborgne R. Tipping Point Leadership. *Harvard Business Review.* 2003

Chater N. The mind is flat. Available from URL: http://www2.warwick.ac.uk/knowledge/business/themindisflat/

(A video lecture outlining the role beliefs play in the decision making process).

Clinical Human Factors Group. Elaine Bromiley Report. Available from URL: http://chfg.org/articles-films-guides/articles/elaine-bromiley-report

(Website with resources regarding the Elaine Bromiley case and situational awareness)

Health and Safety Executive. Reducing error and influencing behaviour. *HSG48*. 1999. HSE Books.

Kahneman D. Thinking, Fast and Slow. London 2001. Penguin.

Kahneman D and Tversky A. Prospect Theory: An Analysis of Decision Under Risk. *Econometrica*. 1979. 47: 263-91

Keynes JM. The General Theory of Employment. *The Quarterly Journal of Economics*. 1937. 51(**2**): 209-223

Krause TR. The behaviour-based Safety process: managing involvement for an injury-free culture. New York 1996. Van Nostrand Reinhold

Mullins LJ. Management and Organisational Behaviour (7th Edition). 2005. Prentice Hall

Ormerod P. Positive linking: How networks are revolutionising your world. London 2012. Faber & Faber

Reason J. Managing the risks of organisational accidents. Ashgate 1997

Salganik MJ, Dodds PS and Watts DJ. Experimental Study of Inequality and Unpredictability in an Artificial Cultural Market. *Science*. 2006. 311: 854-856

Simon HA. A Behavioural Model of Rational Choice. *The Quarterly Journal of Economics*. 1955. 69(1): 99-118

Thaler R and Sunstein C. Nudge: Improving decisions about health, wealth and happiness. London 2008. Penguin